KW-222-616

# Contents

# Acknowledgements

I would like to thank:

My family;

Gateway and Citygates churches for showing me what church should look like and for knowing how to throw a good wedding;

Miranda for encouraging me to write a book;

Toby for his incisive comments on the manuscript in its final stages;

My mum for her diligent and intelligent comments;

All my other friend's who have stood with me over the years;

My Lord and Saviour, Jesus Christ, the inspiration for this book; and

Anna, my wife, my co-conspirator and my friend.

# Prologue

Speaking to many Christians about suffering, I have often wondered if I have got things totally wrong. For where they speak of perseverance, of triumphing over evil and of success in spite of their circumstances, I often see quite the opposite. Things haven't always worked out as I'd hoped for. The tragedies of the past have sometimes had negative repercussions on me and any good that might have come out of them has been insignificant compared to the tragedies themselves.

On first looking to the Bible, I saw that many verses confirmed the view presented by some of my friends as they showed our Biblical heroes triumphing in the face of adversity. For example in the book of Romans where Paul says, "we also glory in our sufferings, because we know that suffering produces perseverance; perseverance, character; and character, hope" (Romans 5: 3–4). But, through further reading, I discovered that there is another darker strand in the Bible that is frequently overlooked. The so-called *dark psalms* express grief and sorrow in the face of suffering, sometimes even a feeling of abandonment by God; the story of Israel and its exile in which the northern kingdom was lost altogether is a devastating tragedy; grief is expressed throughout the Old Testament and the Bible – its epicentre being Jesus on the cross. Though terrible, these stories gave me comfort that perhaps I was not alone in my bewilderment in the face of pain and God.

Lest I appear to rebuke my friends, I must say that they are of course correct that God does indeed bring redemption in this fallen world. Good *can* spring forth in the bleakest of situations. However the good that results does not necessarily answer the challenge posed by the bleakness of the evil from which it springs.

Writing this book, I am concerned with the tragedies of life – tragedies that can appear meaningless and that defy anyone to try to make sense of them. Divorces, murders, rapes, genocides, injustices and illnesses – both mental and physical – can be engaged with by Christians, with God and with the Bible without first having to be justified, explained and theologised. It is the task of this book to dwell in these dark places, as the theologian Jürgen Moltmann once wrote, "to develop a particular theology within earshot of the dying cry of Jesus".[1]

My book is intended to be a personal response to the problem of how we face the evil and suffering that occurs in the world. The holocaust of World War II is perhaps the most notorious example of suffering and evil but it is sadly not alone amongst the world's horrors. On a personal level, I myself have witnessed tragedies both amongst family and friends – events that have brought the problem of evil into sharp focus. Suffering does not have to be dramatic for it to be significant. Our sufferings, as we experience them, can have deep and lasting impacts on our relationships with others and with God.

Discussion of the problem of evil must necessarily be a personal and vulnerable discussion. We absolutely must consider our own suffering when we engage with this problem. Any wrestling with the *Why?* of suffering must also respond to the challenge of its specificity in order to be honest. And so we must ask not only 'why does a loving God allow human beings to suffer?' but also, 'why does *my* loving God allow *me* and *my* loved ones to suffer?' If a response cannot answer these questions then it is only a half answer. Above all, my hope is that this book is an honest response to the evil that I have experienced in my life and that it is able to speak to the pain that you, my reader, have experienced.

John Henry Moule Chamberlain

# Why is evil a problem and what is theodicy?

This is a book concerned with ideas about suffering and about God. The ideas that I consider within these pages have been expressed by many people and with many voices through the ages. Some have contributed original thoughts whilst others have developed or elaborated on what came before. They range in time from the almost pre-historic person of Job, sitting and scratching his sores whilst he berated his friends and his creator; the early church fathers tasked with making sense of the words and life of Jesus; the writers and novelists seeking to make use of their stories to illustrate and investigate the problem; through to the philosophers and theologians wrestling with the secular thoughts of their days. These people range vastly in approach from, what some may find to be, the dry, academic responses of philosophers at one end of the spectrum to the personal, emotional responses of those trying to make sense of their own suffering at the other. All, though, are concerned with one central problem, which is also the concern of this book – the problem of evil. And all their voices can only be secondary to the voices that express the problem best: the voices that cry out into the darkness – those of the victims of suffering.

It is the questions raised by the problem of evil that I am concerned with in this first chapter, for to understand the voices and their conversations, we must first understand what questions they seek to answer. This chapter therefore serves as an introduction to the book by describing the setting in which the conversation takes place. I will also introduce some of the main speakers in the discussion who will appear more fully later on in the book. Hopefully by setting out the broad landscape of the problem itself first, the reader will be aided as they progress through the specific voices and ideas themselves in greater detail later on.

**Evil exists**
To begin, we must first recognise that there is indeed a *problem* and for there to be a problem there must be such a thing as evil which I will define here as being suffering that is without purpose. This book has been written over a number of years, in any of which I could point to terrible tragedies occurring around the world that bear witness to the evil that occurs. Many of the more dramatic events, such as famines or conflicts, have tended to take place in far off countries. However I am not shielded from suffering because I live in the West – though the suffering tends to be of a different sort. Occasionally during my life I have been jerked out of my day-to-day existence and confronted with something appalling. Sometimes it is second hand, when I have witnessed the deprivation of others in my own society or it might be direct, through the death of a loved one or other personal tragedy. Such

events cut into life suddenly like a sharp knife tearing through cloth as I leave my day-to-day life and enter an in-between state whilst I confront the evil that I have encountered.

*The Brothers Karamazov*, by the Russian writer Fyodor Dostoevsky, is a book to which I will return often since its central theme is the problem of evil. A key part of this book focuses on a discussion between Ivan, an atheist, and his brother, Alyosha, a Christian. This discussion concerns the problem of evil and Ivan's role in the conversation is to set out the case against God. Ivan does this initially by detailing various atrocities that have been committed against children – using these as evidence of the existence of evil in order to accuse God of being responsible for this. Dostoevsky is said to have used recent news stories in Russia as his source material for these atrocities – actual events and crimes that had been committed. His point is clear: evil is real and is abhorrent and it forms a case against God. I will discuss this further in the chapter *Ivan Karamazov accuses God*.

In the chapter, *But why me?*, I consider what happens when we meet evil in our own lives. For it is then that the problem of evil is most acute and most personal. The evil and suffering of the world is not spread evenly but falls to varying degrees on different people. It is this particularity that is considered in this chapter.

### So, evil exists, but who is responsible?
If we conclude that we live in a world that contains evil, our next question is naturally, 'Whose fault is it? Who is responsible?' There are two possible responses that we can have to these questions: either we can place the responsibility for this evil on God or we can place it

elsewhere by distancing God as far as possible from the evil that occurs in the world. Different theologians have chosen different answers to this question but if we do give the answer that God is to blame, then what next? Can we shout at God? Can we be angry with God? Or, if we cannot be angry with God, are we still able to be honest with God about how we feel when we suffer?

To tackle this we must consider God as the creator of all things. Since He set things up, does that make Him responsible for everything that happens thereafter? And what about God being viewed as all-powerful? If He is able to prevent evil occurring by intervening, then when He chooses not to intervene to prevent evil, must He also be responsible for the evil that then occurs? The analogy we can use here is that of a person who witnesses a burglary taking place. The witness may have the power to prevent the act by calling the police but they may choose not to do so. Does this make them responsible for the burglary through their failure to act? I will be considering these questions within the chapter *Is it ever alright to get angry with God?*

### If God is all-powerful, all-knowing and good then why doesn't He do something about it?

So, if I conclude that evil exists and God is responsible, then where does that leave my belief in God? Is it a problem? I do believe in an all-powerful (omnipotent), all-knowing (omniscient) and good God who cares intimately about all of our lives. We are His children and He loves us to such an extent that He even knows the number of hairs on each of our heads (Luke 12: 7). So, if He cares so much about us, does that mean that He should prevent us from suffering? In the Gospel of Luke, Jesus compares God to a father who gives good gifts to His children. "Which of you fathers", he asks, "if your son asks for a fish, will give him a snake instead? Or if he asks for an egg, will give him a scorpion?" (Luke 11: 11–12). Is God guilty of giving us, His children, scorpions of suffering? God may not have directly inflicted evil upon us but He has at the very least permitted it to exist in His world and that is why we suffer from it.

Furthermore, not only do we suffer, but suffering does not appear to be distributed in a fair way. It is not only the wicked that suffer. Those who do good suffer also and often to a greater degree. There seems to be a basic injustice to life – an issue that the book of Job is at pains to highlight. The heart of the question is this: as an all-powerful God, surely He could have eliminated evil, or not introduced it into the world in the first place, and surely that would be a good thing? Since He is also a good God, surely He would eliminate evil if he could? And yet evil exists. So, surely He is either not all-powerful or not good or evil does not in fact exist?

David Hume was a Scottish philosopher who lived in the eighteenth century. He was one of the key figures in western philosophy and in the enlightenment. In his *Dialogues Concerning Natural Religion*, Hume sums up the problem succinctly:

> Is He willing to prevent evil, but not able? then He is impotent. Is He able, but not willing? then He is malevolent. Is He both able and willing? whence then is evil?[2]

God in Pain

Or, if you prefer:

> Why is there any misery at all in the
> world? Not by chance, surely. From
> some cause, then. It is from the
> intention of the Deity? But He is
> perfectly benevolent. Is it contrary to
> His intention? But He is almighty.
> Nothing can shake the solidity of this
> reasoning, so short, so clear, so
> decisive.[3]

## The theodicies respond

So, in this world of evil and suffering, where humanity is
tormented and ravaged by horrors, how does anyone
affirm their belief in an all-powerful, good, compassionate
and loving God? How can the Christian withstand the
challenges that evil brings and thus give an adequate
response to the arguments of the philosopher Hume? How
can the Christian engage intellectually, emotionally and
spiritually with the suffering that they see and yet still
worship the God responsible? It is here that the so-called
*theodicies* step in.

The term *theodicy* was coined by the philosopher
Gottfried Leibniz and is derived from ancient Greek. It
could be literally translated as *justice* (or justification –
dike, δικη) of God (theos, θεος). This literal translation of
*theodicy* is illuminating, since it reveals the apologetic
motives of many theodicists in the face of evil as they
sought to justify God.

There are two traditional theodicies that are central to the
argument. Most other theodicies are adaptations of these.
These two theodicies begin from different premises and

are commonly associated with Augustine and Irenaeus, although they have since taken on a life of their own. Each of them has a common-sense aspect and so I will be using accessible forms of the two arguments that are often found in general discussions by Christians, rather than looking at Augustine and Irenaeus' specific views. So let us now see how they aim to justify God.

## Augustine responds: We are all free to do evil

Augustine of Hippo, the early church theologian of the fourth and fifth centuries AD, is commonly associated with a theodicy that is referred to as the *Augustinian defence* but is more commonly known as the *freewill defence* for it hinges on the use of freewill. It is probably the most frequently used theodicy and is the one to which I subscribed when I was growing up. The freewill defence argues that the existence of evil is essentially a by-product of humanity exercising its freewill. So, because I as a free human being was created with freewill, I am free to murder my neighbour which will result in his or her suffering. Hence, unless God intervenes on every occasion to prevent the misuse of my own freewill, then, as an imperfect being, I am bound to commit evil at some point. If I commit evil, then evil exists and so do its repercussions, hence the existence of suffering. Augustine and the freewill defence are discussed further in the chapters *The Grand Inquisitor interrogates Jesus* and *Is evil a price worth paying for the gift of freewill?*

## Irenaeus responds: What doesn't kill us makes us stronger

The second main theodicy is commonly associated with Saint Irenaeus. Irenaeus lived in the second century, some 200 years before Saint Augustine. He was a bishop in what is now Lyons, France. He learned from Polycarp, who was himself said to be a disciple of the apostle John.

Irenaeus' theodicy shares the same perspective as the aphorism 'what doesn't kill us, makes us stronger'. Irenaeus argued that the suffering that we experience improves our souls, refining them for eternity. This *soul-making* defence argues that all the suffering that we undergo is a learning experience that enables us to grow. Without suffering, there would be no challenges and so no need for the altruistic or self-sacrificial love that seeks to alleviate the suffering of others at the expense of oneself. Without our sin and the evil that it promotes, there would be no need for the cross. Since altruistic love and the cross are only possible in a world with suffering, suffering is worthwhile since it brings these about. It was Irenaeus' view that man was made in the image of God but has to be brought into the likeness of God through suffering. For, "man was created as incomplete, 'only the raw material for a further and more difficult stage of God's creative work'"[4]. Irenaeus' response is discussed further in the chapter *God intends all things for good?*

**The Bible: Tension**
As a Christian, it is not just to the philosophers and theologians that I can turn to for help, there is of course the Bible itself, which must be fundamental to any Christian response to such a problem. The chapter *Stubborn Job and his refusal to accept his suffering* seeks to explore what the book of Job says about suffering whilst *The Bible reflects the triple affirmation* explores the other books of the Bible.

One aspect of the Biblical response is that of tension. Henri Blocher gives a good, and thought-provoking description of the Biblical view in his book, *La Mal et la croix*. Written in 1990 and based on a series of articles, it was subsequently translated into English under the name *Evil and the Cross: An Analytical Look at the Problem of Pain*. One of the most striking points that Blocher raises is in his treatment of the Bible. Blocher reflects,

> Scripture raises the triple affirmation: that evil is evil, that the Lord is sovereign, and that God is good, His creation also being good with a similar kind of goodness.[5]

In chapter four, I explore the Biblical basis of these three affirmations and find that they are all maintained and held in tension with each other. It is as if there was a three-way tug-of-war with each truth trying to pull against the other two. When any two of these three truths are combined they create tension with the third as they appear to oppose it. However, the Bible affirms all three. God's goodness and His sovereignty are not of a nature that they prevent evil from existing. God's sovereignty and the existence of evil do not diminish God's goodness. Finally, God's goodness and the existence of evil do not mean that our God is anything less than sovereign. Dwelling on these three tenets can tie our minds in knots, but did we ever expect God to be easy, or even possible, to understand?

Holding this triple affirmation is challenging, and it is precisely this challenge that is the task of theodicies to explain and so to diminish it whilst, by contrast, the Bible holds these seeming contradictions in tension, without compromise. The Bible asserts that, as in other areas, if something is true then it is true, no matter how difficult this might be to comprehend. This is not a call to irrationalism but a call to dwell in the paradox and seek to learn from it rather than to seek to resolve it and thus end the discussion. As for irrationalism, I will later return to the issue of logic to consider whether these three truths are illogical when taken together, especially since they are strikingly similar to the philosopher Alvin Plantinga's statements that are discussed in the chapter *The philosophers discuss.*

Interestingly, the Augustinian freewill defence is an attack on the sovereignty of God for it deals with what God is able to do. The defence argues that God is not capable of creating a world with freewill but without evil since evil is essentially a by-product of freewill. Does God's inability to do so mean that He is not sovereign or is it simply a logical impossibility and so irrelevant to God's sovereignty? On the other hand the Irenaean soul-making defence is an attack on the existence of evil, since if suffering has the purpose of improving us, then surely it is not evil. Hence both defences jar with the Biblical account, which holds all three truths uncompromisingly in tension. It is this tension, and the underlying unease with which any defence of God must be treated, that underpins this book. To restate Blocher's point in his own words,

> The thorn in reason's flesh ...the evil
> of evil, the lordship of the Lord, the
> goodness of God: these three
> immovable propositions stand together
> as the basis of the Biblical doctrine.[6]

### A discussion and a story

Many of the key texts that I will introduce later in this book use conversation as a technique to engage with the problem. The book of Job; the discussion of evil between

Ivan and Alyosha Karamazov; and Elie Wiesel's trial of
God all demonstrate how the problem of evil finds its best
expressions not as a dry set of statements, but through
narrative and discussion. It is the conversation between
God and humanity; between one person and another, that
enables us to comprehend the problem. Additionally,
stories allow for nuance, grey areas and are open to
interpretation which is vital when a definitive answer may
not be appropriate.

For this reason I have framed this book as a discussion
between parties; for the most part humans for, just as in
the book of Job, the discussion of evil takes place largely
between Job and his friends over thirty-five chapters
whilst God's response, out of the storm, is a mere four
chapters, so in this book it is people that dominate the
discussion. The chapter *The shouting of the voices* seeks to
bring together the different strands of the discussion by
reviewing what the writers, theologians, philosophers and
victims have said. By introducing the stories of Job,
Dostoevsky and Wiesel, I seek to use narrative to speak
where mere teaching can only be silent.

The final discourse implicit in this book is that between
the reader and the book itself and the story is that of the
reader's life. I am aware that suffering is a deeply
personal, important and delicate issue for many readers.
Many will bring their own narratives to this book, whether
of personal suffering or intellectual exploration and my
hope is that the narratives and discussions here will
resonate with each reader to enrich and enhance their own
stories, rather than to deny or silence them.

**The ugly great ditch**

It strikes me as unusual for a subject to be discussed, in depth, in academic theology and philosophy as well as devotional theology. Usually these areas do not coincide since they are focused on different issues and have different priorities. The academics dismiss merely *practical theology* for the masses as being anti-intellectual whilst the rest of us may view the academics as being obscure people who debate over the number of angels that can dance on the head of a pin. In theodicy though, there is a subject in which the interests of both groups converge.

Nevertheless, there does exist an *ugly great ditch*. For although this is a subject that is capable of academic discussion, its subject matter is deeply personal and emotional. Theodicy is a problem that can be expressed in both philosophical and emotional language and the confusion between the two is the cause of the ditch. The philosophical language stands on one side of the ditch and emotional language on the other. The two languages shout to each other but fail to communicate properly due to their differences in vocabulary and intentions.

On the philosophers' side of the ditch we have the logical problem: if God is all-knowing and all-powerful, and entirely good then why does evil exist? On the other side of the ditch we have the emotional problem: how could You let this happen? Do You really love me? And yet You watch me suffer!

This ditch is recognised by many writers. John Hick, the philosopher and theologian, states the issue well when he says,

> The problem of evil is an intellectual problem about agonizing realities, and probably no one who has not first agonized in their presence is qualified to think realistically about them in their absence; but nevertheless the agonizing and the thinking are distinct, and no amount of the one can do duty for the other.[7]

I will use two books written by C.S. Lewis on suffering to map out the breadth of this ditch. I have huge admiration for C.S. Lewis as a writer whose honesty, integrity and intellect comes through in his profound works. For our current purposes I will be referring to his books *The Problem of Pain* and *A Grief Observed* – two works that stand on opposite sides of this ugly great ditch.

In 1940, C.S. Lewis wrote *The Problem of Pain*, an excellent attempt to wrestle with the same questions as this book, but from an intellectual, detached standpoint. C.S. Lewis was acutely conscious of this fact and indeed discussed it in the preface. He had originally wanted to publish the book anonymously as he felt that his book did not reflect his life. His publisher refused his request and so they compromised by allowing him to include a preface in which he detailed his reservations:

> the only purpose of the book is to solve the intellectual problem raised by suffering; for the far higher task of teaching fortitude and patience I was never fool enough to suppose myself qualified, nor have I anything to offer my readers except my conviction that

> when pain is to be borne, a little
> courage helps more than much
> knowledge, a little human sympathy
> more than much courage and the least
> tincture of the love of God more than
> all.[8]

*The Problem of Pain* therefore stands firmly on the logical side of the ditch whilst recognising the vast gulf that exists between it and, what I have called, the *emotional side*. Many years later, in 1961, C.S. Lewis wrote *A Grief Observed*. As with *The Problem of Pain* he initially intended for it to be published anonymously though, unlike his earlier work, he was successful in this and so, in 1961, it was published under the pseudonym N.W. Clerk. His reason for desiring anonymity on this occasion had changed; this book was deeply, deeply personal. It dealt with the death of his wife, who he referred to as *H*, and his mourning for her. It is a moving book and I would recommend it to any reader. In it, C.S. Lewis writes of his loss and how he has struggled to come to terms with it. He speaks of his anger at God and how he despairs in his loss and suffering. He doesn't try to conceal his anger with God and doesn't back away from the sorrow that he is experiencing but instead details it at length. The reader is given an intimate portrayal of this process.

Whereas his former book speaks of theodicy intellectually, this book does not even attempt a theodicy. What is the result? I regard *A Grief Observed* as a demolition of the ideas in *The Problem of Pain* for they do not stand up to C.S. Lewis' own experiences on the other side of the ditch – when confronted with personal tragedy. Just as he foresaw in his preface to *The Problem of Pain*, the arguments of the past were not able to help C.S. Lewis in his grief. As we shall see in the chapter *Stubborn Job and his refusal to accept his suffering*, Job refused to accept the intellectual response to evil, and so C.S. Lewis imitates him as he also rages against his Creator. Indeed, after one such rant he says "I wrote that last night. It was a yell rather than a thought"[9]. As a reader, I can only feel sympathy for his yells – pain hurts and when we experience it we suffer and want to yell and rant and rage against God. To deny such thoughts, to suppress them, as C.S. Lewis unfortunately did in *The Problem of Pain*, can be unhelpful.

We are therefore left with the ditch. One side is cold and logical and so does not, indeed cannot, speak to us in our grief; the other side is emotional and is a response of tears. Is there a way to speak into the pain, does God provide comfort to us in our distress? Or to rephrase the question: what book could C.S. Lewis have written in 1940 that would have spoken to him twenty-one years later in 1961?

It is interesting to note that another author, Timothy Keller in his book *Walking with God through Pain & Suffering*, takes the step of dividing his book into three with the different parts sitting on different sides of the ditch. For him, the divide is between the philosophical and the theological, which form two parts of his book (*Understanding the Furnace* and *Facing the Furnace*) and sit on the logical side of the ditch, and the devotional (*Walking with God in the Furnace*), which sits on the emotional side. His words here are helpful,

> ...not all of us are currently in an experience of deep pain and grief. Those who are not feeling it, but are seeing it in others, will have a host of

> philosophical, social, psychological, and moral questions about it. On the other hand, those who are in the grip of pain and difficulty *now* cannot treat it as a philosophical issue.[10]

I hope that I am not "fool enough" to seek to teach fortitude and patience to those in suffering, but it is also my, perhaps foolish, hope that this book can bridge the ditch between *The Problem of Pain* and *A Grief Observed* and thus be philosophical and theological as well as devotional. I am seeking to speak into the pain and suffering that all experience. I am seeking to address both the mind and the soul.

# The philosophers discuss

The problem of evil is a subject that impacts both philosophy and theology. Philosophers set the background and pose the questions that must be answered whilst the theologians provide details. It is the philosophers that are considered in this chapter. They come from very different backgrounds and perspectives. Firstly there is David Hume, the Scottish enlightenment philosopher who portrays the problem of evil using an artificial dialogue between three fictional characters, each with a different philosophical standpoint. Next is Alvin Plantinga, the twentieth-century philosopher of religion who approached the subject using the technical language of logic. Whilst Hume and Plantinga provide an overview of the subject, Archbishop William King is the last philosopher that I will discuss on my whistle-stop tour. He considered the definition of evil from a philosophical perspective and identified three types of evil. All three philosophers held views that are illuminating for our discussion.

**David Hume converses**
Since ancient times many philosophers have used staged dialogues to describe ideas and how they interact with each other. In these dialogues different, usually fictional, characters discuss a philosophical issue, with one character being a proponent of one viewpoint and another character proposing a contrary view. The dialogue is a useful tool in describing all aspects of an argument and it is one that I have sought to draw upon in my book. David Hume made use of this approach in his *Dialogues concerning natural religion*, which discussed, among other things, the problem of evil.

The dialogue on the problem of evil spans two parts of Hume's overall dialogue (X and XI).[11] It is a wide-ranging discussion – a summary of which is included in Appendix I to this book. The three characters involved in the discussion do not reach a consensus on the problem of evil and so I am not able to say definitively here what Hume's view of theodicy was but instead will draw out a few of the points of the discussion. Firstly, one of the characters, Philo, argues that the existence of evil in the world is incompatible with the existence of a God who is good in a human sense. An all-powerful and good human would surely not allow some of the great tragedies that have happened in the world and so, since God is all-powerful, He cannot be good in the way that we understand the word. There is a similarity between this view and the theodicy that justifies suffering by referring to *God's mysterious ways*. But, in response, if God is so mysterious and if His goodness is so different to our idea of goodness then this raises the question of how we can know Him?

Secondly Hume sets a thought experiment: what would a universe look like that was created by a good God? Philo argues that it would look very different to our own universe which contains too much suffering to be created by a good God. I discuss this later in my chapter, *The problem of good*, where I come up with my own experiment.

Finally, four different circumstances in which evil arises are discussed. All of these circumstances should be preventable by an all-powerful God and so evil should be preventable. But, in that case, why doesn't He prevent it? Why didn't He set things up differently so that we would not suffer? Philo concedes that there could be an unknown explanation for why all four circumstances are somehow necessary but this feels like an unsatisfactory response. Can we be satisfied with an explanation that we do not, and maybe cannot, know?

**Let's get logical**
Next we turn to Alvin Plantinga and his logic, which cuts to the heart of the issue at hand. Plantinga was an American philosopher of the twentieth century who wrote extensively on the philosophy of religion. Among his many books, he wrote *God, Freedom and Evil* in which he examined the formal logic of the problem of evil. In this, he sets forth statements, which if true logically either prove or disprove that a good God is consistent with the existence of evil. Please note that he does not attempt to prove the existence of God, merely that God's existence is not illogical. His argument is therefore a defence of God's existence rather that an argument *for* God's existence. Plantinga begins his argument with statements 'a' and 'b' that, between them, summarise the Bible's triple affirmation:[12]

    (a)   God is all-knowing (omniscient), all-powerful (omnipotent) and entirely good.

    (b)   Evil exists.

Statements 'a' and 'b' set out the issue. If 'a' and 'b' are logically inconsistent then God's very existence is logically impossible and we should all join Richard Dawkins and his atheist friends. To argue in favour of their consistency Plantinga argues that the statement 'c' below is consistent with 'a' and that when taken together with 'a' logically implies 'b'. This statement is:

    (c)   God creates a world containing evil and has a good reason for doing so.

In other words, if there is a good reason for evil to exist then a good, all-powerful God may exist also. To take the step further than the logic of Plantinga, I would add that belief in a loving and all-powerful God together with the existence of evil necessitates a belief that God *must* have had a good reason for creating the world as it is. Plantinga has elegantly got to the heart of the issue here. Believers must assert that 'c' is true in order to believe in both 'a' and 'b'. So, is 'c' possible? Could God have a good reason for creating the world as He has done?

The non-believer can only counter 'c' by saying that God could not possibly have a good reason for this. Such an attack though is open to the response that an all-knowing God could have reasons that are completely beyond human comprehension, but still good. Without claiming omniscience, the sceptic has no counter to this for they cannot know all the possible reasons that there could be for creating a world with evil and so they cannot disprove them though they may feel unsatisfied just as they did on hearing Philo's arguments above.

Plantinga uses the analogy of *noseeums*, tiny almost invisible flies, to illustrate this point,

> [If I look inside a tent and] I don't see a St. Bernard [dog]. It is then probable that there is no St. Bernard in my tent. That is because if there were one, it is highly likely that I would have seen it. ...Again I look inside my tent and I don't see any noseeums. ...This time it is not particularly probable that there are no noseeums in my tent. ...The reason is that even if there were noseeums there I wouldn't see 'em; they're too small to see. And now the question is whether God's reasons, if any, for permitting such evils ...are more like St. Bernards or more like noseeums. ...Given that He is omniscient and given our very substantial epistemic limitations, it isn't at all surprising that His reasons ...escape us.[13]

Hence it is entirely possible that there is a good reason for the existence of evil that we are unaware of. So do we believe that God has such a reason? The problem of evil all seems to boil down to whether we trust God and His purposes.

Two such reasons are contained with the freewill and soul-making defences. Both assume that 'c' is true. In the freewill defence, God's good reason for evil is that it is an inevitable by-product of freewill and the assumption is therefore that the existence of freewill and evil is better than no freewill and no evil. We could even argue that having no freewill is an evil in itself of sorts. In the soul-making defence, the good reason for the existence of evil is the development of a good soul, which it facilitates.

Although Plantinga has successfully used logic here to argue the case, he also recognises the presence of the ugly great ditch and the limitations of philosophy when he says,

> neither a Free Will Defence nor a Free Will Theodicy is designed to be of much help or comfort to one suffering from such a storm in the soul ...Neither is to be thought of first of all as a means of pastoral counselling. Probably neither will enable someone to find peace with himself and with God in the face of the evil the world contains. But then, of course, neither is intended for that purpose.[14]

## Archbishop King and his three types of evil

William King was Archbishop of Dublin in the Church of Ireland in the early eighteen century. In his *An Essay on the Origin of Evil*, he identified three types of evil. John Hick described these in his book, *Evil and the God of Love*.[15] The first type is evil related to imperfection. For King, created beings cannot be as perfect as their Creator but must instead be less perfect because, in the world of cause and effect, an effect must be inferior to its cause. Hence, the evil of imperfection is unavoidable. Alongside Leibniz,[16] King argues that God has created a world that has the least imperfections possible and so, although it is imperfect, it is still the best of all possible worlds. King then argues that the other two types of evil flow from this imperfection.

The second type of evil, natural evil, is inevitable in a universe that has matter in motion. Matter must be in motion to contain living creatures and this motion, amongst imperfect objects, will inevitably lead to clashing, opposition and repulsion – hence natural evil. Furthermore, the location of souls within physical bodies leads to creatures experiencing physical pain, which they need in order to avoid danger. God has tried to minimise the amount of suffering caused by this by setting things up such that we live in the best of all possible worlds.

Finally, moral evil is identified as the third type of evil and King uses the freewill defence to explain it. As we are free to sin and we are imperfect, we choose to sin – hence moral evil. King then looks at why God gave us this freewill, given the inevitable outcome of our sins and suffering. He provides two complementary answers, firstly the universe would be defective without the existence of freedom to a greater extent than it is defective with sin. Secondly, freewill provides "room for covenant and mutual love".[17] Without freewill we cannot truly love nor can we faithfully enter into promises to one another or to God.

Another distinction can be made when looking at evil. Plantinga showed that the role of theodicy is to provide a good reason or purpose for suffering and evil. Senseless suffering, such as the premature death of a loved one, requires theodicy to provide an explanation. On the other hand, some suffering has a purpose that is already apparent regardless of theodicy. For example, where an illness causes suffering but is later healed and leads to a strengthening of character in the sufferer's later life. Such suffering is not necessarily evil but may instead be an outworking of good.

## The New Atheism is preoccupied elsewhere

Given the prevalence of concerns about the problem of evil as a popular attack on belief in God, it is interesting to note that the subject does not appear to be a major concern for the so-called *New Atheists* such as Richard Dawkins and Daniel Dennett. Indeed, Richard Dawkins once wrote, "I have never found the problem of evil very persuasive as an argument against deities"[18]. This may be partly because their attack is an attack on all belief in God and so they seek to caricature God as evil and then attack belief in this evil God. An evil God is of course compatible with the existence of evil, but not of good. Or perhaps it is that they view the problem of evil as an emotional, rather than a logical, attack on the existence of God and agree with Stephen Davis when he says that, "[the logical problem of evil] is no longer credible as an objection to theism".[19] Davis' bold statement is in large part down to the above-mentioned work of Alvin Plantinga, which seems to have shifted the scholarly debate. So, if Plantinga has addressed the academic side of the ditch then how does that help us when we are sitting on the other side?

John Henry Moule Chamberlain

# Stubborn Job and his refusal to accept his suffering

## My initial confusion

I had always felt confused by the book of Job in the Bible. On considering suffering, it was the first book that sprang to mind and yet every time I read it, I felt that I was missing the point. Whilst researching my own book I returned to Job and in particular the narrative of the argument between Job, his friends and finally God. This argument makes up the majority of the book but it is not something that I had ever got to grips with previously, perhaps due to its length and because, on a cursory reading, it appears to repeat the same points again and again and so is confusing.

In Appendix II, I have summarised the discussion in chapters 3 to 42 of the book of Job. Spending time doing this greatly aided my appreciation of the book since it gave me a better understanding of how the conversation flowed and the points that each speaker was trying to make. For those who also struggle to understand the book of Job I would encourage them to read this Appendix or even to write their own summary and therefore to gain a richer understanding of what, I have now come to realise, is a magnificent book.

What then did I learn from my time with Job? This chapter details the story of the book of Job and what it tells us about the problem of evil.

**The stage is set**
The book of Job begins with a story, which runs through two parallel narratives. The first narrative is that of the life of Job, a man who lived many years ago in the land of Uz. From the first verse he is described as being "blameless and upright, he feared God and shunned evil" (Job 1: 1). As will become clear further on in the book, these words are to be taken literally – Job is without sin. Job lives a contented life, with seven sons and three daughters as well as a large number of livestock.

Having introduced Job, the book then turns to the second narrative – in the heavenly courts where God is looking down on Job and boasts to Satan about Job's blamelessness (Job 1: 8). It is almost as if God is a proud parent who looks on fondly at his child and cannot help but boast about him. Satan, of course, has other ideas and challenges God that Job is only good because God has blessed him with many riches and much favour – without these Job will surely curse God (Job 1: 11). God then allows Satan to try to cause Job to suffer on the condition that Satan must not hurt Job himself (Job 1: 12).

The wager here is, I believe, a narrative device and is not intended to imply that God really places bets with Satan and allows suffering in order to win those bets. Rather the wager can be viewed as a metaphor for the struggle with evil and suffering that we all undergo as God's creatures, with God seeing the best in us and Satan seeing the worst.

The story next moves back from the heavenly courts to the life of Job where the impact of Satan's work is seen. One day Job is approached by three messengers, each of whom report the death of Job's livestock and servants (Job 1: 14–17). Then a final, fourth messenger arrives to report the death of Job's children who had been feasting nearby (Job 1: 18–19). At this, Job is disconsolate, he tears his clothes and shaves his head to mark his mourning and then falls to the ground in worship and says (Job 1: 21):

> Naked I came from my mother's womb,
> and naked I shall depart.
> The Lord gave and the Lord has taken away;
> may the name of the Lord be praised.

Job has therefore defeated Satan's wager through his response for he has not cursed God but has instead praised Him. The story now shifts back to the heavenly court where God and Satan again discuss Job. Satan's view of Job appears to have been discredited and so he ups the stakes by demanding to be allowed to harm Job's body also in order to try to make Job curse God (Job 2: 5). God consents and so Satan goes out and afflicts Job with painful sores (Job 2: 7). Job, crushed, takes a piece of pottery to scrape his sores and sits among the ashes of his former home. His wife encourages him to curse God and die but Job refuses (Job 2: 9–10).

At this point, Job's three friends, Eliphaz, Bildad and Zophar, arrive, seeking to comfort him:

> When they saw him from a distance, they could hardly recognise him; they began to weep aloud, and they tore their robes and sprinkled dust on their heads. Then they sat on the ground with him for seven days and seven nights. No-one said a word to him, because they saw how great his suffering was.
> (Job 2: 12–13).

What follows this period of silence, for the next forty chapters, is a conversation between Job and the three friends together with another, Elihu. Eventually God joins the conversation and concludes it. Whilst Job is insistent that he has not sinned and so is not deserving of the suffering that he has experienced, the friends seek to explain his suffering by claiming that he must have sinned and so deserves to suffer. There are two main arguments that the friends use, in some ways they can be seen as two different theodicies – justifications of God in the face of suffering.

### First theodicy: Job's suffering is as a result of God's loving discipline

The friends' fundamental assumption is that Job must be at fault for otherwise he would not be suffering and this they state right from the start ("Who, being innocent, has ever perished? …those who sow trouble reap it", Job 4: 7–8). Job's friends propose that his suffering is as a result of God's loving correction for a sin that Job has committed.

One example of this theodicy of the friends is spoken by Eliphaz in Job 5: 17:

> Blessed is the man whom God corrects;
> so do not despise the discipline of the Almighty.

Note the added wound that Eliphaz inflicts by saying that Job should not despise his own suffering but rather that he is blessed by it. This reprimand uses the metaphor of the father and child, which is implied by loving correction. Just as a parent may seek to teach their child through correction, so does God. This is a theodicy that we hear in various forms today – maybe God is trying to test us so that we might grow through our sufferings.

## Second theodicy: Job's suffering is God's punishment for Job's sins

As the argument becomes more heated, Job's friends' theodicies become more condemnatory. Now they argue that Job's suffering is not as a result of God's loving correction but as a punishment for Job since he is wicked. Zophar uses this attack in Job 20: 23 & 29:

> When he has filled his belly,
> God will vent his burning anger against him
> and rain down his blows upon him
> …Such is the fate God allots the wicked,
> the heritage appointed for them by God.

God in Pain

Absurd as it sounds, given our belief in a God of love, this is still a very common belief today – the sense that people 'get what they deserve'. I remember a non-Christian friend once expressed this view to me as he found the world crashing down around him whilst facing an unjust potential criminal conviction. Justice was eventually done and he was found innocent but I wonder whether, having gone through this period, he still maintains his *faith* that people 'get what they deserve'. Job protests his innocence to this attack. He is not deserving of such punishment. However this initially meets the deaf ears of his friends – perhaps Job has committed a sin of which he is unaware, they ask.

Underlying this reprimand is a key assumption – that the universe is fair *within our lifetimes*. Hence, God will exercise his divine judgement within our lives to ensure that all the wrongs and injustices that are committed on earth are punished. The Biblical teachings about judgement day and the need for restoration in the afterlife imply that such a belief is incorrect. If they leave any doubt then the book of Job reinforces the point. The universe is not just, hence the need for the cross and for judgement day.

These two defences both seek to give reason to suffering where sometimes there is no reason – suffering is sometimes truly senseless. It is natural that we, as human beings, seek to make sense of the events of our lives and to give meaning to them however the flaws of both these theodicies teach us that sometimes meaning and purpose simply cannot be given.

**God's response**
Perhaps the most remarkable thing about the book of Job is God's speech. From chapters 3 to 37, Job and his friends have been discussing Job's suffering. They have argued and argued over why God has let this happen to Job. Job has incessantly accused God of punishing him unjustly whilst Job's friends have defended God. The argument seems to go around in circles and become more and more heated as they squabble over who is right and who is wrong. Job is now not only suffering for his losses and injuries, he is also angry. He is angry with God and angry with his friends. As things seem to have come to an impasse, the missing, but most important party to their conversation joins in – God.

Initially God appears to side with Job's friends by accusing Job of using "words without knowledge" (Job 38: 2). Where was Job at the creation of the world when God set all in motion (Job 38: 4)? God challenges Job to respond to him (Job 40: 2) and Job timidly responds, "I am unworthy – how can I reply to you?" (Job 40: 4). Job's friends must have been sitting smugly listening to God and awaiting their affirmation by their Creator as God continued to admonish Job from "out of the storm" (Job 40: 6 – 41: 34). They must have felt vindicated and the argument won as they watched Job appear to repent, "Surely I spoke of things I did not understand" (Job 42: 3). But then a strange thing happens when God, having rebuked Job, says to Eliphaz, the first of Job's friends to have spoken, "I am angry with you and your two friends, because you have not spoken of me what is right, as my servant Job has." (Job 42: 7). I wonder, if it had not been for the storm, how loud the sound of a pin dropping must have sounded at that moment. Although God has admonished Job for his words, He has saved His harshest rebuke for those that were trying to defend Him and accuse Job. He has even said that Job's words were right.

And so, it is at this point that God says, as He does throughout the Bible, for all time, that 'I am with you. I am with the victims. I am with the persecuted and downtrodden. I am not with the accusers of others but I am with those who seek to contend with me'.

## The outcome – restoration

After God's response ends the argument there follows a brief epilogue that takes us back to the story of Job's life and his restoration. Firstly, Job prays for God to forgive his friends for their misspoken words and God accepts Job's prayer (Job 42: 9). Job's role as mediator here prefigures the role that Jesus will take as mediator between humanity and God. Job is then comforted by his brothers and sisters and other friends (Job 42: 11). Job's family and wealth are restored and increased as he has another seven sons and three daughters and eventually he dies, "old and full of years" (Job 42: 17).

This epilogue shows the restoration of Job, as we will all be restored in heaven. It does not however remove the significance of the suffering that Job underwent and it does not diminish the importance of the chapters that preceded it. The message of the book of Job is certainly not that it's okay because we will all live happily ever after. Rather, the message is that suffering is real, that it matters, that God cares and that there is the possibility of restoration.

## Not a theodicy!

A theodicy is literally a justification of God in the face of evil and so a person who proposes a theodicy is trying to stand as a defender of God – just as Job's friends tried to do. The book of Job is therefore resoundingly not a theodicy though it is easy to fall into the trap of mistaking it for one and so misunderstand the purpose of the book. Through contemplating the book of Job, I gradually came to the realisation that the book is not seeking to justify God but instead to restate the problem of evil and to dwell within it.

Throughout the book, Job accuses God, for Job holds to two truths – first, that he is righteous and second, that his suffering is therefore unjustified. Standing on these two truths, Job accuses God, for God is all-powerful and so it would be within God's power to prevent Job's suffering. How, Job asks, could God allow this to happen to him? Job's friends respond with theodicies that seek to defend God.

Henri Blocher observed that, when confronted with the triple affirmation that God is good, that God is all-powerful and that evil is evil, "[Many] Christian thinkers ...have obscured, rejected even, one or another of them".[20] Job's friends have essentially responded in the same way – in their case they have argued that Job's suffering is not in fact evil. Rather the friends are arguing that Job's suffering has a purpose – either to punish him or to lovingly correct him – and if it has a purpose then it is not evil but good. On first reading the book of Job, I was initially in line with his friends for I was expecting to hear, I thought that I needed to hear, a justification. How is suffering and evil justified? Why do we have it and why do we hurt so? But Job himself says nothing other than to insist on the truth of his claims and the injustice of his situation and, he argues, the injustice of God. Job himself states the problem but does not offer a solution, instead he demands an answer from God, "I desire to speak to the Almighty, and to argue my case with God" (Job 13: 3).

Eventually God appears and so as readers we expect that at this point there will finally be an answer – a theodicy. However God does not provide a theodicy when He instead sides with Job, not with Job's friends. This is something that I have struggled with for a long time but I may now be starting to understand it. The book of Job is not a theodicy; theodicies are expounded by Job's friends as they try to defend God from Job's attacks and they are rebuked for this. Rather, the book of Job, is a statement of the problem *as a problem*.

That it is a problem is vitally important because if it were not a problem then it would mean that one of the three strands was incorrect – either evil is not evil, God is not sovereign or God is not good. The book of Job affirms, by way of Job's justified protests, that it *is* a problem, for evil does exist. What's more, it is a problem for God also and God is intimately concerned with this problem. He is not however concerned with the problem in order to justify His own role in it for He had the opportunity to do so in the book of Job and chose not to. Rather what seems to concern God is the impact of evil on the people that He loves.

### The book of Job allows us to ask questions
God is a God of relationship and perhaps the most remarkable thing in that relationship is that, despite the immense distinction between the two parties, God listens and allows people to participate in that relationship as if they were equals. The God of the Bible seems to welcome certain challenges by people. This is most obviously shown in Genesis 32 when Jacob wrestles with God. In

this story, Jacob is alone one night. A mysterious man then appears who wrestles with Jacob. They wrestle as equals with neither of them overpowering the other but Jacob's hip is dislocated. At day-break the man wants to leave but Jacob will not let him go without a blessing. Eventually the man blesses Jacob, renaming him Israel, which means 'he struggles with God'. When questioned, the man refuses to give his name and leaves but after he has left Jacob names the place Peniel, which means 'face of God', since it was the place where he saw God face to face and yet lived. Jacob was the father of the nation of Israel and so this story serves as a prophetic image of the nation of Israel's relationship with God. Israel will be allowed to meet with God *face to face* and live. It will be allowed even to wrestle with God, as if with an equal, and live. This wrestling will not be without consequences, as shown in the injured hip, but equally it will not be without blessing from God. Turning to Job, we have a continuation of this tradition of questioning, for Job is not content to suffer without crying out to and challenging his Maker: How could God let this happen to him? Why is this happening?

We are children of God and as His children we are in relationship with Him. It is quite right that this parent-child relationship involves questioning. If a child is disciplined by her mother then it is right that the child understands the reason for the punishment rather than suffering in confusion. In fact if the child does not understand any action of her mother then the mother would of course far rather that the child asked her for her reasons rather than simply remain in ignorance. Likewise I think with our Father in heaven. When we suffer, when things in our lives do not turn out as we hoped, I think that God would far rather that we question Him and talk to

God in Pain

Him rather than just shrug our shoulders with vague thoughts of His *mysterious ways*. We must of course always be respectful of the awesome power and love of God, but this does not mean that He expects us to remain silent when we are confused or hurt.

Bishop Handley Moule was the bishop of Durham from 1901 to 1920 and was also my great-great-great-uncle. In one of his books he described a related quality, which Job also displays – that of not suffering in silence. Going against the idea of stoicism, Handley says when talking about Paul's thorn in the flesh:

> He [Paul] records the repeated entreaty [to God] without any regret, with no trace of a feeling that he ought to have endured in silence ...'Learn to suffer without crying out', is a noble precept – as regards 'cries' to man, which are often better forborne. But the maxim has no bearing upon cries to God, to the Christ of God. Too ready, too outspoken, too confiding, we cannot be in 'telling Jesus all'. Such 'crying out' will not weaken us; it will only strengthen us. For it is the outgoing of our soul not only to infinite wisdom and strength. It is taking refuge in the Rock.[21]

**These questions don't always need answers**

*Night* by Elie Wiesel is a book that also reflects upon the problem of evil and is perhaps influenced, through the Jewish heritage of the author, by the book of Job. *Night* is about the author's experiences in Auschwitz as a prisoner.

I will be returning again to this magnificent work but for now I want to touch briefly on it. At the start of the novel Wiesel describes life in Sighet, a village in Romania where he lived up until being forced into a Jewish ghetto and eventually into the concentration camps. One of the characters in this early part of his life was Moishe the Beadle, a down and out, who befriended the thirteen year-old Wiesel. Moishe the Beadle was a master of the Jewish form of mysticism, Kabbalah, and in the book *Night*, he explained to Wiesel that, "every question possessed a power that was lost in the answer..."[22] The idea, that it is questions, and indeed unanswered questions that are important, that matter, rather than their answers, not only frames the novel *Night*, but should, I think, be central to any consideration of the problem of evil. It is vital to ask the questions, and sometimes we must refrain from giving answers, which might close down the questions.

I, like Wiesel and Job, would seek to ask questions when confronted with suffering and even to allow these questions to live and breathe and be. Only when space for the questions has been allowed can we seek, not to answer them, but to respond and address the issues that they raise, whilst not diminishing them. Many responses to suffering seem to close down the questions and this is a trap that we would seek to avoid. The book of Job likewise, by not providing a theodicy, allows us to continue the conversation.

Paul Bradbury, in his moving account of his own suffering through the parenting of his sick child in the book, *Life from Death Emerging*, clearly appreciates the importance of questions, not answers when he describes "resting in the unknown"[23] and goes on to say that, "Sometimes knowledge is nothing more than noise that fills the quiet space in which God dwells. Without that knowledge we are able to dwell there too in silence".[24]

As Job himself says to his friends, "Have windy words no limit? Or what provokes you to keep on talking?" (Job 16: 3). Perhaps we should bear this in mind when seeking to comfort others. Sometimes words are not required, nor are answers sought after, instead we should just dwell with people in their suffering and so instead help in some small way by our mere presence rather than antagonise them by seeking to explain their circumstances.

## Nevertheless Job's friends give their answers

This is a lesson that Job's friends could learn. Initially though, their actions are good for, at the outset on hearing of Job's distress, like supportive friends they arrive in order to comfort him (Job 2: 11–13). On seeing his distress, they weep with him and spend seven days and seven nights sitting with him in silence. In Jewish tradition there is the concept of "Shivah" (שבעה), which is literally translated as "seven" and refers to the week-long mourning period after the death of a close relative. This practice follows the story of Joseph's period of mourning for the death of his father Jacob in Genesis (50: 1–14). Sitting in Shivah represents a transitional stage for the mourner as they come to terms with the death of their relative. I once heard a sermon on the subject of the book of Job. This sermon made the point that sitting in Shivah was probably the best thing that Job's friends could do for him; to sit and to weep with a friend, to participate and share in their suffering, is perhaps the best that we can do as friends. Unfortunately, as with Job's friends, it is when we open our mouths that we often get things wrong. We should heed the truth of the proverb by not answering suffering with words (Proverbs 25: 20). Job's friends are not only using words where none are needed, they are even trying to speak on God's behalf, as Elihu at one point says, "there is more to be said on God's behalf" (Job 36: 2). We have no reason to doubt their intentions or motives in this. So why is it that when God joins the conversation, it is Job's friends who are corrected rather than Job? To introduce the answer to this question we will turn to another part of the Bible.

2 Samuel 6: 3–7 (repeated in 1 Chronicles 13: 9–12) tells the unfortunate story of Uzzah and the Ark of the Covenant. The Ark of the Covenant was representative of the presence of God on earth and was extremely holy as well as being fearsome. Indeed, God explicitly commanded that the Ark should not be touched (Numbers 4: 15). This story takes place before the temple had been built and so the Ark of the Covenant travelled around on a cart pulled by oxen. At one point in its travels, the oxen stumbled and so Uzzah, who was escorting it at the time, reached out and took hold of the Ark to prevent it falling. For this, Uzzah was struck down dead by God.

This is one of those passages that is difficult to read and understand. Why did God punish Uzzah? To answer this we must first note that the passage says that the oxen had stumbled but does not say that the Ark was slipping. Uzzah's action of reaching out to steady the Ark betrays a view that Uzzah had that the Ark needed help, that it would fall without his help. However, the Ark, as the embodiment of holiness, did not need help and so Uzzah's act was blasphemous. He was seeking to help the Ark and therefore God, as if God needed his help. A similar sin might be someone who says words of comfort to a friend but then claims that these words are from God. The words of comfort may be helpful but that does not allow the comforter to claim the authority of God. Indeed, such authority is unnecessary when the truth of such words may be self-evident. No matter how well intentioned we may be, we should never seek to take the place of God. We should never try to do His job for Him since such acts deny God's competence to act and so are highly offensive.

Writing this, I am struck by how difficult it must be to be in God's position. Countless people claim to speak and act on His behalf. Many of them do immense damage in this whether directly, in such acts as the tragedy of the crusaders, or indirectly through well intentioned and even good acts that, when attributed to God, can lead to a false impression of God in the recipient. For instance, if we comfort a friend who is struggling with singleness with the words, 'God has great plans for you' then we might give false hope, which ultimately could lead to despondency and the blaming of God. We should be very cautious in attributing words to God.

Turning back to Job and his friends, the friends were corrected by God for seeking to answer on His behalf. They thought that they were speaking for God, they sought to close down Job's questioning and struggling but perhaps it was this questioning that God wanted to hear. I think that God is big enough to take our questions and concerns, our troubles and fears, He does not need to be defended by Uzzah or anyone else.

I am highly conscious in writing this book of the gross error that I could make in this area. Any writer of a theodicy should beware of falling into the trap into which Job's friends fell of seeking to answer for God when no answer is given by God. Perhaps that is the point of any true theodicy, there is no answer, only silence. But it is a

silence that stands alongside us and with us. It is a silence *HT*
that weeps also. Hopefully, the reader will conclude that
this book falls on the right side of the line in how it
approaches the issue. The response of this book is
intended to be the same as that of Job's friends in those
first seven days, but I may err if I go beyond.

## The answers of Job's friends inevitably cause distress for Job

Throughout the book of Job, Job pleads with his friends to
cease their words, which only bring further pain to him
and estrange him from them. To give one example, in Job
19: 2, Job says "How long will you torment me and crush
me with words?" Rather Job desires pity, "Have pity on
me my friends, have pity" (Job 19: 21) he pleads. I am
reminded of a famous remark commonly attributed to
Saint Francis of Assisi: "Preach the gospel at all times and
if necessary use words". The point is that we all too often
seek to use words to solve a situation, desperately
searching for the right thing to say, but if we are to mourn
with those who mourn, do we really need words?

## Job yearns for Jesus

I am not alone in that when I am angry or upset I say
things that I later come to regret – things that I don't really
mean. For all of us, our thoughts tend to be diverted in
unhelpful and sometimes hurtful ways when we are
speaking from emotion. Fundamentally, we are not
reasonable and far less are we rational in these situations.
In a similar way, we are capable of experiencing the same
irrationality when we are hoping or dreaming for
something – so-called 'flights of fancy'. This is when we
dwell on a dream and allow our minds to enhance and
extrapolate the dream.

But just imagine if, in one of these moments of emotional unreasonableness, we happened to hit upon something, some deep profound truth. Something so significant that it would impact on all of humanity and something that was previously unknown. It seems extremely unlikely of course but this is just the thing that happens in the book of Job.

Throughout, Job insists that he is righteous and yet he suffers. Job attributes the blame for his suffering to God. He maintains that God has therefore wronged him (Job 19: 6) and so he is left frustrated by the fact that he cannot take God to task for this (Job 19: 7). Job yearns to be able to do just that – to face the one who has wronged him as if in court (Job 13: 3). But how can a mere man contend with God Almighty? Who can face God and accuse him? Job seems to have a flash of revelation in chapter 16 when he says:

> Even now my witness is in heaven;
> My advocate is on high.
> My intercessor is my friend
> As my eyes pour out tears to God;
> On behalf of a man he pleads with God
> As a man pleads for his friend
> (Job 16: 19–21)

Who is this advocate in heaven? These words, to Job's friends, must have appeared as if a vain hope. He develops this hope further in Job 19: 25 when he says "I know that my Redeemer lives, and that in the end he will stand upon the earth". This Redeemer, this intercessor, is of course Jesus, who would walk the earth centuries later and who pleads our case in heaven (1 John 2: 1).

This prophecy is quite staggering. In the book of Job, possibly one of the earliest books written in the Bible, we are presented with a man suffering greatly. He talks with his friends in extremely emotional, personal language about his pain and suffering – how God has wronged him and he wants God to take the blame for it as if in court. He wants God to restore him. And then he talks as if he, a mere man, has an advocate, a Redeemer in heaven who will plead his case for him. Foolish, vain words of hope. And yet hundreds, if not thousands of years later, there comes to earth just the man of which he has spoken. Just the man that Job longed for. But not only that, this man not only pleads our case, he also takes our place and takes the punishment for our sins. Job's hope was more than fulfilled in Jesus.

## The point we often choose to ignore

The one last point that I would like to make about the book of Job arose from a conversation with my sister. We were discussing Job and I tried to summarise its message. I concluded that there is probably one basic point – 'bad things happen to good people'. I am struck, the more I think about it, by how important it is to understand this point. It's the point that we are most prone to get wrong, whether we are religious or not. I think this is due to some fundamental and natural human prejudices as it seems to be an innate tendency in people. It is a sense of natural justice that my non-Christian friend had and that was the basis of Job's friends second theodicy – that people 'get what they deserve', a form of karma. We see how in the Gospel of John, Jesus' disciples are still getting it wrong when they attribute a man's blindness to sin (John 9: 2). We also see Jesus making the same point when describing a tragedy of a collapsed tower that killed eighteen people

– it was not their sin that led to their deaths (Luke 13: 4–5).

In my own life, I often think that the misfortunes and suffering that I experience are as a result of my own sin. This is not a theological or rational thought and it is not one that has ever been taught to me, but I still feel it. There must be something deep down in our psyche for us to feel this way – perhaps it is as a result of our fallen, sinful nature. Sometimes we are disciplined by God and we must use discernment and wisdom to identify these times and respond accordingly. The story of Job makes it plain though – even if you are without sin, you will still suffer and bad things will still happen to you. Do not believe the scoffers, friends or your own thoughts that tell you that it is your own fault. Job did not believe his friends and he was vindicated by God in this.

Thinking of my tragedies and those of my loved ones, I can turn to the book of Job and see that bad things do happen to some of the very best of people.

# The Bible reflects the triple affirmation

From the book of Job, I now turn to what some of the other books of the Bible have to say about the problem of evil. This is not an attempt to give a complete exposition of the Biblical portrayal of the subject – such a task would fill many volumes of books. Rather I make use here of Henri Blocher's aforementioned triple affirmation and consider its Biblical basis – the affirmation that God is all-powerful, that God is good and that evil exists and is *evil*. Having reviewed some of the verses, which affirm these statements, I will then briefly look at some of the other books of the Bible that also consider the problem of evil.

### God is all-powerful

The first two affirmations of Blocher's triplet seem so fundamental to Christianity that an in-depth argument to their Biblical basis is unnecessary. Nevertheless, it is always good to question the root of any Christian truism.

God in Pain

Turning firstly to God's powerfulness, the first verses that are relevant are those that use the name El Shaddai ( אל שׁדי) to refer to God. This occurs many times in the Bible with its first appearance being in Genesis 17: 1 ("When Abram was ninety-nine years old, the Lord appeared to him and said, "I am God Almighty [El Shaddai]; walk before me faithfully and be blameless"). Many Bible translations, such as the New International Version just quoted, translate El Shaddai as "God Almighty" for it is a title that refers to the all-powerfulness of God.

Looking at the overall Biblical story we see that God's powerfulness is regularly emphasised in the narrative through the stories of miracles, which suspend the laws of nature, of resurrections of the dead and of His power to save. Perhaps the primary example of God's power is that of the creation in Genesis 1. Whatever lessons we learn from this story, one must be that God's power cannot be limited by this world since He is the Creator and shaper of it. Pertinent to this book is that God created the universe to be a certain way and, as Creator, He surely could have done differently and instead created it another way. However, He chose to create it as it is. The Bible confirms this for, when God had completed His creation, He saw that it was good (Genesis 1: 31). The other side of God's power though is shown by the story of the flood in Genesis 6 where God demonstrates His ability to destroy the world – that which He created.

God's power is also illustrated in the book of Job where, in chapters 38 to 41, God speaks of His own power and contrasts it with that of Job. "Where were you when I laid the earth's foundation? ...Have you ever given orders to the morning, or shown the dawn its place ...Can you bind the beautiful Pleiades? Can you loose the cords of Orion?

Can you bring forth the constellations in their seasons?" (Job 38: 4, 12, 32). Referring back to creation and also God's role as sustainer of the universe, God emphasises His own power in comparison to the comparatively insignificant power of humankind.

## God is good

The Bible tells us that God is good. No complicated argument is needed here since the belief that God is good is at the very core of the Bible. As Blocher remarks, "The testimony to the perfect justice and goodness of God is one of the constants of Scripture".[25] Perhaps the verse that portrays this most simply is 1 John 4: 8 which includes the words "...because God is love" but it is not so much specific statements about God that form our belief in the goodness of God, rather it is the grand sweep of the Biblical story where God demonstrates His love and goodness, not through words, but through actions. On the cross, by sacrificing His only son to save His human children, God demonstrated just how far He would go for His love of us – there was no limit. This is the love that convinces us of the goodness of God.

## Evil and God in the Bible – two views

The third of Blocher's affirmations, that evil exists and is evil, requires more consideration than the first two for the Bible's view of evil is more nuanced. Hick argues that, "There are, then, two attitudes to evil within the Bible, one based upon the dualistic view of evil as the irreconcilable enemy of God and man, and the other upon a profound sense of the sole ultimate sovereignty and responsibility of God."[26] It is these two views that comprise the tension contained in the Biblical portrayal of evil. I would argue however that both of these views affirm the triple affirmation – the former focusing on the evilness of evil alone whilst the latter affirms both the evilness of evil and the powerfulness of God.

Hick cites several places in the Bible, which portray this latter view of evil in which God is in control such that all evil that happens is in accordance with His will.[27] Firstly, at the start of the book of Job, there is the ambiguity of the court scene where God allows Satan to harm Job and so seems to permit evil which implies that he could also forbid it. Next Hick refers to the book of Isaiah where God says, "I form the light and create darkness, I bring prosperity and create disaster; I, the Lord, do all these things." (Isaiah 45: 7). Hence the Bible implies that God has a role in both the good and the evil that befalls people. Lamentations follows a similar path, "Is it not from the mouth of the Most High that both calamities and good things come?" (Lamentations 3: 38). Amos is starker by attributing disasters to God, "When a trumpet sounds in a city, do not the people tremble? When disaster comes to a city, has not the Lord caused it? (Amos 3: 6).

How can we reconcile such verses with belief in a good God? We need to be very careful in how we interpret the verses because at times in the Bible God uses disasters to punish a nation,

> 'I am about to summon all the peoples of the northern kingdoms,' declares the Lord. 'Their kings will come and set up their thrones in the entrance of the gates of Jerusalem; they will come against all her surrounding walls and against all the towns of Judah. I will pronounce my judgments on my people because of their wickedness in

forsaking me, in burning incense to
other gods and in worshiping what
their hands have made.' (Jeremiah 1:
15–16)

Hence, to call such a disaster evil is misleading for an evil
disaster would surely be without purpose or meaning.
These verses affirm that God may be behind some
suffering however they also raise the question of whether
such suffering is evil. As Job's friends found out, there is
an important distinction made by the Bible between
suffering that is discipline from God and suffering that is
needless. It is important, in all cases, to seek to discern
between the two.

Turning to the dualistic view of evil as the 'irreconcilable
enemy of God and man', as Hick points out[28], most books
of the Bible contain verses that point to God's abhorrence
of evil. Amongst these, Hick cites Isaiah 13: 11, "I will
punish the world for its evil, the wicked for their sins. I
will put an end to the arrogance of the haughty and will
humble the pride of the ruthless." Also, as with its proof of
God's love, the cross is also the proof of the evilness of
evil for God thought it worth sacrificing His only son in
order to defeat it.

The first three chapters in the Bible, in the book of
Genesis, are the story of where evil originally began. At
their heart is the triple affirmation: God's all-powerfulness
is affirmed by His creation of the world in Genesis 1 and
His ability to plan the coming of Jesus and the final defeat
of Satan by the serpent crusher from the beginning
(Genesis 3: 15); the evilness of evil is affirmed by the
need to banish Adam and Eve from the Garden of Eden
(Genesis 3: 23); God's goodness and love is affirmed by

His creation of Adam and Eve and the Garden of Eden and that even after they had sinned He still assisted them by clothing them (Genesis 3: 21).

It would also be worth mentioning here that the fall of Adam and Eve in Genesis 3 is perhaps the strongest Biblical argument in favour of the freewill will defence. Adam and Eve chose to eat the apple that God had warned them not to eat and as a consequence of their own free choice they were banished from the Garden of Eden and suffered as a consequence. Hence the story of the fall is the story of how evil entered into the world through the free choice of Adam and Eve.

## The Bible and the story of Israel

I often read the Bible whilst travelling on tube trains in London. In doing so, rather than prayerfully contemplate each verse, I instead read the Bible at the same pace that I would any other book. This means that I inevitably miss much of the deeper meaning of each passage but, in place of this loss, I gain an understanding of the overarching story of the Bible and how it all fits together. This has led me to discover that one of the themes of the Bible, and in particular the Old Testament, is that of one nation trying to come to terms with the defeat and suffering that seems to defy the earlier promises of God.

The Old Testament tells the story of the rise of a nation – the Israelites. They are a blessed nation whom God favours. They are unlike any other nation because, rather than an earthly king, they have God as their king. To begin with though the Israelites did not see themselves as a nation since they began, in the book of Exodus, as a mere group of slaves living in Egypt. Through the miraculous intervention of God and the prophetic leadership of

Moses, the Israelites were able to flee Egypt into the desert in search of the land that God had promised them – a land where they could set up a great kingdom. In the book of Joshua, they finally moved into the land, conquered it and settled in it having wandered in the desert for years.

This should have been the start of the happy ending however it was not. The nation initially succeeded in its new home but its people soon started to call for human kings to rule over them rather than God. God granted them their wish however the change seemed to hasten their demise as, after the rule of just three human kings, the nation was divided into two – Israel and Judah. Israel was in the north and ruled by one king whilst Judah was in the south and ruled by another. Eventually, the Assyrians conquered both the northern and southern kingdoms and took many of the Israelites into their own empire. After that the northern kingdom of Israel was lost apparently forever and the southern kingdom of Judah remained only as a remnant of its former self. Next the Babylonians conquered Judah and destroyed the temple where the Israelites had worshipped God. All seemed lost as the Jews found themselves worshipping their God, under threat of persecution, in Babylon. Eventually a few returned to Judah and rebuilt the temple but it was a mere shadow of its former glory. The greatness of Judah did not return to the heights that it had reached previously and the kingdom of Israel in the north seemed lost forever.

My potted history of the Old Testament cannot do justice to the human tragedy that occurs when kingdoms rise and fall – I have not mentioned the murders, the rapes and the torture that a conquering army carries out. It is into this tragedy that the prophetic books speak. They try to make sense of the disaster that has befallen Israel, where the promises of God appear to have been broken as death and defeat lies all around them. The early prophetic books are written before the exile and warn Israel of the judgement that is to come, if they continue to turn away from God and seek to worship other gods. Later, after the exile to Babylon has occurred, the prophets try to make sense of what has happened and why God appears absent in this tragedy. Finally, there is hope as the prophets point to a future restoration and a Messiah – a new king.

Four hundred years separate the Old and New Testaments. Four hundred years of a nation defeated as, despite struggles for freedom, the Jews now find themselves ruled by another empire – the Romans. It is onto this landscape that the feet of Jesus walked. It is Jesus' death on the cross and inauguration of the church that completes the story of the Bible – a story of suffering. The cross represents the culmination of all the suffering that has preceded it as God steps into the drama and suffers with His people. The cross also represents the defeat of this evil as Jesus triumphs over it through his resurrection.

They say that, 'history is written by the winners' – the Bible is not. The Bible tells the underside of history – the story of a nation that appeared to be beaten. It is, perhaps, for this reason that it is so helpful for the problem of evil since it is written by those who, in the midst of suffering, consider their faith in God.

## Suffering: a thread running through many books of the Bible
Many of the books of the Bible reflect on the loss that Israel has suffered. Lamentations is one such book as it tries to make sense of the situation. It was written in

Jerusalem after the city had fallen to the Babylonians. It portrays the grieving of a nation for its loss and, like the book of Job, it asks questions of God and His role in the situation.

The book of Habakkuk also reflects on suffering. It is written in the form of a conversation between Habakkuk and God and, echoing Job, it begins with Habakkuk's complaint to God that He has not intervened to prevent the injustices being done. Habakkuk laments the prosperity of the wicked, whilst God assures him that justice will be restored.

In the book of Ecclesiastes, it is the suffering and injustice of the weak in everyday life amidst the prosperity of the wicked that, amongst other things, leads the Teacher to begin by booming, "Meaningless! Meaningless! ...Utterly meaningless! Everything is meaningless" (Ecclesiastes 1: 2). In chapter 4 the Teacher focuses specifically on the suffering of the oppressed,

> I saw the tears of the oppressed—
> and they have no comforter;
> power was on the side of their oppressors—
> and they have no comforter.
> And I declared that the dead,
> who had already died,
> are happier than the living,
> who are still alive.
> But better than both
> is the one who has never been born,
> who has not seen the evil
> that is done under the sun.
> (Ecclesiastes 4: 1–3)

The Teacher in Ecclesiastes concludes at the end that the only response to this meaninglessness is to cling to the eternal, where order is restored and meaning can be found,

> Now all has been heard;
> here is the conclusion of the matter:
> Fear    God    and    keep    his
> commandments,
> for this is the duty of all mankind.
> For God will bring every deed into
> judgment,
> including every hidden thing,
> whether it is good or evil.
> (Ecclesiastes 12: 13–14)

Many different passages could have been used here to demonstrate the Bible's comments on evil and suffering, but hopefully this has given a brief glimpse of the character of the Bible in its reflections on suffering – a character that is honest, pensive and moved by suffering. In doing so, the passages raise more questions than they answer and so bring a challenge to us and our faith in God.

**Psalm 107 and the causes of suffering**
When I was young I was a member of a church youth group which had inspiring leaders – Kevin, Gill and Alex – who helped nurture my faith. Kevin and Gill were a married couple and were both bikers. Kevin seemed to always be working on a bike in his garage. They were the first bikers that I got to know and I remember a period of a few weeks after meeting them when I seemed to see motorbikes everywhere I went. Now this was not, I assume, because of a sudden influx of motorbikes in London, it was simply that I had started to notice what had always been there. The process of writing this book is

similar, I am seeing theodicy everywhere and Psalm 107 is one such example.

Psalm 107 lists several categories of people, all of who cry out to the Lord in their suffering. Firstly (107: 4–9) are those who wandered in the desert and were hungry and thirsty. They cry out to God in their distress and God shows the way to a city. There is no explanation given for this group's suffering, but it is an obvious reference to Israel's desert wanderings. God's plan for Israel was for them to travel through the desert to the promised land. This journey would no doubt involve some hardship but it was prolonged by Israel's disobedience. We can therefore suggest from this reference, that this is a group of people who are suffering as a result of following God's plan – albeit the suffering is compounded by their own disobedience.

Next (107: 10–16) are those who sat in darkness having rebelled against God. They are described as prisoners in chains. Their misery is a result of their rebellion against God leading to God giving them bitter labour and allowing them to stumble without help. It is as if God has hidden His face from them and permitted them to put on these chains. Like the first group though, when they cry out to God, God brings them out of the darkness, breaks their chains and restores them.

Next (107: 17–22) we encounter those who are suffering from affliction through rebelling against God. When they cry out to God He brings healing. The final group of people (107: 23–32) are seafarers who sail far and wide. God brings a tempest against them and in their distress they cry out to God and He rescues them. Here we have suffering being brought, not as a result of disobedience, but it seems as a test from God. This section of the psalm prefigures the story of Jesus and the calming of the storm in the Gospel of Mark (Mark 4: 35–41). The story of the calming of the storm teaches us that God is ultimately in control, even in periods of distress. The seafarers are right to call out to God but their calling out also betrays a lack of faith. They know where to turn when in need, but they don't necessarily trust that God will supply their needs without being asked.

Perhaps the central message of this psalm is one that is fundamental to the Bible's view of suffering. No matter what our circumstances, whether our suffering is our own fault or the fault of others, we can cry out to God and He will respond.

### Saint Paul: hope in suffering

Finally, when we turn to the letters of Paul in the New Testament, we find a slightly different view of suffering that nevertheless follows on from the earlier despair of the Bible's laments. Paul establishes a clear link between suffering and hope, a link that is expressed in Romans (5: 2–4), "And we boast in the hope of the glory of God. Not only so, but we also glory in our sufferings, because we know that suffering produces perseverance; perseverance, character; and character, hope." God's love and the work of the Holy Spirit strengthen believers so that they can experience hope, not just as an anticipation of the future but with a very real impact today. This hope does not remove suffering in the present but brings a new, fresh perspective to it that enables it to be better endured.

N.T. Wright wrote about Paul's view of suffering. For Wright, suffering in Paul is not just a producer of hope but goes further and is, in a sense, redemptive for he argues that God saves His people "not despite their sufferings but through and even because of them. Somehow ...the sufferings of God's people are taken up into God's purposes."[29] Wright's statement is a nuanced version of the soul-making defence. Similarly, Roger Forster, the theologian and church leader, argued that endurance of suffering is a fundamental Christian principal that is found "all over the New Testament".[30] Arguing this, Forster cites John 16: 33, Ephesians 6: 13 and Hebrews 10:35–39 as examples.

By linking suffering with hope and redemption, Paul is not only writing words of encouragement to his readers but is also picking up on a theme in the Old Testament. Many Old Testament prophets, such as Isaiah, point to a future hope through the coming suffering servant Messiah who will bring redemption. It is this hope in God that brings comfort to the oppressed and is a response to much of the protests of the prophets. The question remains whether it removes the need for protest and absolves God of blame or whether there is still a space for protest? We consider one of the most vociferous protestors in the next chapter – Ivan Karamazov.

God in Pain

John Henry Moule Chamberlain

# Ivan Karamazov accuses God

I was first introduced to the great Russian writer, Fyodor Mikhailovich Dostoevsky, by my brother when he was reading *The Idiot*. *The Idiot* is a book where the character described as *The Idiot* is a Christ-like figure. The comparison of Christ with a so-called *Idiot* intrigued me and reminded me of 1 Corinthians 3: 19 ("For the wisdom of this world is foolishness in God's sight"). Dostoevsky lived from 1821 to 1881, in a period when Russian literature was in its golden age and he and Tolstoy were at the vanguard of this. He was a giant in the world of literature and such was his popularity that as many as 100,000 people are said to have attended his funeral.

My reading of Dostoevsky would eventually take me to what is perhaps Dostoevsky's most revered work – *The Brothers Karamazov*. This tells the story of three brothers: Alyosha – a novice at a monastery; Ivan – a rationalistic atheist who would have been at home in conversation with

59

Hume's Philo;[31] and Dmitri – a man of passion and a sensualist. The novel is a philosophical one, which contrasts the brothers and their different world views against the background narrative of the murder of their father. Its main subject is the problem of evil and there are two central chapters around which this theme pivots – *Rebellion* and *The Grand Inquisitor*. Contained within these chapters is a conversation between the Christian, Alyosha, and the atheist, Ivan.

In the chapter *Rebellion*, Ivan uses the problem of evil to accuse God and describes suffering in all its horror. *The Grand Inquisitor* chapter, although also narrated by Ivan, represents a response to this onslaught in the form of a parable, which explicates as well as attacks, the freewill defence. *Rebellion* will therefore serve as the introduction to this chapter, in which I seek to lay the case against God. I will turn to *The Grand Inquisitor* and explore it in further detail in the following chapter.

### Ivan's rebellion

In the midst of the turmoil that occurs in the story of *The Brothers Karamazov*, Alyosha visits his brother, Ivan. To Ivan, Alyosha is representative of Christianity, and so, as a passionate atheist, Ivan launches into an attack on Christianity. Alyosha says little and the vast majority of the dialogue in these chapters is spoken by Ivan. Ivan's speech is in the mode of a, perhaps drunken, rant.

Ivan commences his speech by saying that, "I never could understand how it's possible to love one's neighbours"[32]. This may have been possible for Jesus, but he is God and Ivan is not. The difficulty with loving one's neighbours, Ivan argues, is that, for example, they may smell or have a foolish face – "It's still possible to love one's neighbour abstractly, and even occasionally from a distance, but hardly ever up close"[33]. These opening remarks show Ivan's mind-set at the start – he struggles with this fundamental Christian principal and his inability to accept it shapes his views that follow.

Ivan then turns to his main concern, the suffering of mankind in general and, in particular, the suffering of children. Children, unlike adults, can be loved up close whereas adults, for Ivan, cannot. Furthermore, adults have knowledge of good and evil and have eaten the apple of the Garden of Eden and so are not innocent. Why should innocent children therefore suffer for the sins of their fathers?

Ivan goes on to describe stories of immense suffering that have occurred, starting with the atrocities that the Turks were said to have committed in Bulgaria. For much of the nineteenth century, Bulgaria was ruled over by the Ottoman Empire. The ruling Turks feared an uprising by the Slavic people and so are reported by Ivan to have committed crimes that have an animalistic cruelty. Indeed, Ivan remarks that to call these acts animalistic would be an insult to the animal kingdom, since no animal could ever be as cruel as man. Ivan describes babies being cut from their mother's wombs, tossed into the air and skewered with bayonets in front of their mothers. As an *amusing* trick, Ivan alleges that the Turks would toy with a baby whilst it was held by its mother. The baby would of course laugh as they cooed it but then they would point their pistol four inches from the baby's face. The baby would naturally reach for the gun, thinking it a toy, at which point the perpetrator would pull the trigger in the face of the infant.

Ivan relays several other stories of suffering perpetrated by one person on another. His final story is perhaps the most shocking. Dostoevsky found this story recorded in a Russian periodical at the time[34] – the use here of a *true* story demonstrates Dostoevsky's concern to give a factual account of the barbarity mankind is capable of, rather than a merely fictional portrayal, which would achieve lesser resonance and import. The tragedy is that Dostoevsky does not lack for examples and we are no different today in the stories that we could tell.

Ivan's story takes place on the estate of a wealthy Russian General. In those days, serfdom was still prevalent in Russia and this General had 2,000 such serfs on his own estate. One day the General saw that his favourite dog was limping and so made enquiries to try to find out what had happened. The General discovered that a house-serf, an eight-year-old boy, had thrown a stone whilst playing and this had hit the dog and caused the injury. As punishment, the General ordered that the boy be taken from his mother and locked up for the night. In the morning, the General rode out on his horse, in full dress along with his wolfhounds and huntsmen. The boy was stripped naked and the General gave the order for him to be driven away. Shortly afterwards, the General let loose his pack of wolfhounds and they hunted the child down and tore him to pieces.

Having related this and the other stories, Ivan has a moment of pensiveness. He confesses that he doesn't understand why it's all arranged as it is and then seems to propose the free will defence by saying: "So people themselves are to blame: they were given paradise, they wanted freedom, and stole fire from heaven, knowing that they would become unhappy – so why pity them?"[35].

However, Ivan doesn't accept this since he feels the need for justice.

Ivan then gives a portrayal of the Christian heaven where God's forgiveness of both may allow the victim and the murderer to embrace and cry out together, "Just art thou, O Lord". Ivan doesn't want such a reconciliation because the injustices committed are too severe – he wants judgement. He does not want a *higher harmony*, he wants revenge on the perpetrators, now, not later. He says,

> I absolutely renounce all higher harmony. It is not worth one little tear of even that one tormented child who beat her chest with her little fist and prayed to 'dear God' in a stinking outhouse with her unredeemed tears! Not worth it, because her tears remained unredeemed. They must be redeemed, otherwise there can be no harmony. …Can they be redeemed by being avenged? But what do I care if they are avenged, what do I care if the tormentors are in hell, what can hell set right here, if these ones have already been tormented? …And if the suffering of children goes to make up the sum of suffering needed to buy truth, then I assert beforehand that the whole of truth is not worth such a price. I do not, finally, want the mother to embrace the tormentor who let his dogs tear her son to pieces! …I'd rather remain with my unrequited suffering and unquenched

> indignation, *even if I a wrong*.
> Besides, they have put too high a price
> on harmony; we can't afford to pay so
> much for admission. And therefore I
> hasten to return my ticket. …imagine
> that you yourself are building the
> edifice of human destiny with the
> object of making people happy in the
> finale …but for that you must
> inevitably and unavoidably torture just
> one tiny creature, …and raise your
> edifice on the foundation of her
> unrequited tears – would you agree to
> be the architect on such condition?[36]

Alyosha responds, softly, that he would not agree. Alyosha speaks of Jesus and his forgiveness, which brings Ivan on to his poem of *The Grand Inquisitor* and his encounter with Jesus that we will discuss in the next chapter. Given the severity of the crimes committed, Ivan's attack on God is formidable, his challenge to Alyosha to return his ticket, goes unanswered. How can we respond to descriptions of such suffering? With words?

### Theodicy of protest

Ivan Karamazov's speech is in the tradition of protest as a theodicy – or perhaps an *anti*-theodicy. This tradition views protest against God as a natural response to the problem of evil and, like Ivan, demands to hand back its ticket. The book, *Encountering Evil. Live Options in Theodicy*, presents five different theodicies, each of which is proposed by a theologian. The theologians then critique each other's theodicies and so the book unfolds as an interesting dialogue in which the theologians debate the problem of evil. In Stephen T. Davis' critique of the protest theodicy of his fellow theologian, Roth, Davis argues,

> I think his deepest reason for rejecting eschatological schemes that redeem all evil is not that he thinks it cannot be done. ...I think Roth already does, at least partly, believe that it is within God's power to do it. He may even partly believe that God will do it. But I now see that he thinks the deepest problem is this: to embrace such schemes is to fail to have solidarity with the victims and sufferers. It is to allow their screams of pain to be muted. To retain this solidarity is one of Roth's strongest desiderata in theodicy. And that desire, in my view, is to be accorded nothing but the honour and respect it deserves.

> But real solidarity with the victims and sufferers is telling them the truth. And the truth is that the Christian message of hope through the love of God as expressed pre-eminently in Christ is good news for all people, even those who suffered and died unjustly, maybe especially for them.

Davis' critique here is telling, but not decisive. It is a call for a balance to be struck between protest and the redemptive outcomes that may occur after suffering.

## The right to forgive?

It is notable that none of Ivan's descriptions of suffering refer to his own life. Instead he seeks to portray an *idealised* form of suffering – the suffering of the innocent. Ivan's intent here is appropriate and yet it is also flawed. By describing these extremes of suffering he is bringing a definitive case against God which must be answered. The events that Ivan describes are not fictional but are based on real events and so it is entirely appropriate that Ivan charges God with these. As I have discussed elsewhere, any response to suffering must be capable of responding to its most extreme forms.

The flaw in Ivan's examples is that he does not own them. Just as he is in no position to forgive the perpetrators of these crimes since he is not the victim, he is also in no position to forgive God for allowing them to happen. Only the victims can forgive the perpetrators – that is their right and theirs' alone. The inability of bystanders of suffering to forgive often leads them to self-righteous outrage, as is the case here. A victim can see the good in even the most extreme forms of suffering. They can reflect and dwell on their suffering and, as they do so, can grow in it, reorder their view of it and ultimately move on. A bystander however may end up trapped in the tragedy itself. It is very difficult for them to see beyond this event to its consequences, whether good or bad, since they are often unaware of the final outcome and the true impact on the victim. Even if they were fully aware, they could not judge in the way that a victim can. Divorces can lead to happy remarriages, murders can lead to radical social action, and political prisoners can become presidents. The bystander though often remains focused on the divorce, the murder or the injustice when considering suffering. John Hick remarks, "As has often been observed, in the case of human suffering the intellectual problem of evil usually arises in the mind of the spectator rather than in that of the sufferer".[37] Even Ivan Karamazov recognises the issue of forgiveness mid-way through his rant when he refers to the mother of the murdered child,

> She dare not forgive him! Let her forgive him for herself, if she wants to, let her forgive the tormentor her immeasurable maternal suffering; but she has no right to forgive the suffering of her child who was torn to pieces, she dare not forgive the tormentor, even if the child himself were to forgive him![38]

It is therefore helpful to always consider our own suffering, alongside that of others, when wrestling with this subject. Our own suffering keeps our considerations reasonable and grounded. If we can live with a God who allows our own suffering then what right do we have to take on another's suffering and not accept Him because of that? The extreme cases of the suffering of others should always be considered alongside our own with the answer to them being the same as the answer to our own.

**A modern-day Ivan Karamazov doesn't lack tragedies**

What then are the extreme examples of suffering that a modern day Ivan would lament? In the eighteenth century, the standard example raised by the intellectuals of the enlightenment was the Lisbon earthquake. In terms of human lives lost, this was one of the most destructive natural disasters of all-time, killing up to 100,000 people. Indeed, Voltaire used it as one of the examples of suffering in his book, *Candide*.[39] How could God allow such a thing to happen? Perhaps the modern equivalent of such a devastating natural disaster would be that of the tsunami, which hit the Indian Ocean in 2004. This disaster dwarfed the Lisbon earthquake in its level of destruction with more than 230,000 people in 14 countries losing their lives and countless more being impacted through the loss of homes and loved ones. Joseph Stalin is said to have justified mass murder with the words, "The death of one man is a tragedy, the death of millions is a statistic". Yet God knows the exact number that died in these disasters. He knew every single one of them personally and each one is a tragedy to Him.

One crime looms largest in the modern consciousness as an example of the evil and suffering that has devastated the lives of millions in the world and that still has repercussions to this day. That is the tragedy of the holocaust when eleven million were murdered – Jews, Slavs, gypsies, the mentally ill, the physically disabled, resistance fighters, homosexuals and other people that the Nazis saw fit to eliminate. The eleven million included one million children.

I once visited the concentration camp Auschwitz-Birkenau. It was a bright and sunny day when I arrived with my friend Brenda at this scene of genocide. The sheer scale of the suffering that took place in there was impossible to take in. The museum tried to assist by exhibiting the suitcases, complete with names written neatly on the sides, as well as the shoes of those who had arrived there. It tended to be individual, personal images that impacted most. I was immensely struck by a photograph of a Polish resistance fighter who was being marched into the camp. He must have been in his early twenties and I could see the defiant pride on his face as he strode in with armed guards accompanying him. I always wondered how long he was able to maintain that brave face.

As Elie Wiesel, a concentration camp survivor once wrote, "Never shall I forget those moments that murdered my God and my soul and turned my dreams to ashes."[40]

A response to suffering must be within sight of the gates of Auschwitz.

## Tesie

An example of suffering that is more personal to me is that of Mary E.E. Moule, who was the daughter of Bishop Handley Moule, my great-great-great-uncle. Mary, also known as Tesie, was born in 1882 and died at the age of 22 in 1905. She had lived a life marred by the physical suffering that eventually led to her death. Handley, coming to terms with the loss of his daughter in 1905, wrote *The School of Suffering. A Brief Memorial of Mary E. E. Moule*, dedicated to her memory.

The book tells the story of Tesie's life as she struggled with terminal illness. Her decline is drawn out over the course of her adolescence and early adulthood. Tesie was acutely aware of how much she was missing out on as she watched her sister, Isabel, grow and enjoy all the pleasures that a fit and active life should provide, whilst Tesie herself wasted away. Reading the book, I felt a real sense of the struggle within Tesie as she shifted between two possible responses to her suffering. On the one hand, there was her solid and heroic *Christian* response as she sought to triumph in the midst of her suffering. In contrast to this, the book refers to, but does not describe, her bouts of depression as she struggled to come to terms with her situation. Handley has faithfully recorded both responses of Tesie. I was tempted to view the first response as Tesie trying to make her parents proud and the second response as revealing her true feelings when the veil was removed – however such an interpretation would be unjust. My belief is that Tesie's responses are signs of her trying to understand her own awful situation.

As with C.S. Lewis's *A Grief Observed*, Tesie's book gives a deeply personal description of someone's suffering. Through this, Tesie had several profound insights into Christian suffering. She once reflected that, "it is 'better to walk in the dark with God than to walk alone in the light'"[41] and, "speaking of the strange wreck of her life, [Tesie] said, 'The cross is sharp'"[42]. As with Ivan Karamazov's accusations, the story of Tesie's life could also be used as an attack on God, however Tesie refused to let that happen. By walking with God in the darkness, by understanding the sharpness of the cross, she instead triumphed over suffering, even when this triumph was manifested in the form of depression.

On 18 August 1905, Tesie wrote to a young friend what was to be her last ever letter. It is a moving outpouring of Tesie's heart and is a suitable conclusion to this chapter before we return to Ivan's dispute.

> I must send you this line to say a very loving good-bye. It will be the last thing I shall write, I think... We have drawn together once, with the Lord Jesus as 'the Third between us', and so our friendship must last. He is calling me now to His presence. It is such rest, too wonderful to realise...

Do take Him to your heart, for your *inseparable* Friend. Life is a poor starved thing without Him at its very best. But with Him it will be a glorious thing – whether in prosperity or failure. Not religion, but Jesus Christ, is necessary for you. ...How I should like to see you! But we shall meet again. I believe I shall know about you, and *rejoice* in your life.[43]

God in Pain

John Henry Moule Chamberlain

# The Grand Inquisitor interrogates Jesus

**The parable: the Grand Inquisitor and Ivan accuse**
Following on from the previous chapter in *The Brothers Karamazov*, Ivan Karamazov continues his rant to his brother, Alyosha. Ivan has written what he calls a poem, but which more closely resembles a parable. This parable is titled *The Grand Inquisitor* and is set during the days of the Inquisition in sixteenth century Seville, Spain. In the popular imagination in Russia in the time of Dostoevsky, the days of the Inquisition were seen as a brutal and inhuman saga in world history. The Inquisition began in twelfth century France and was set up to combat heresy within the Roman Catholic Church. This was carried out through holding trials of alleged heretics and burning to death many of those that the Inquisition deemed to be guilty. This was a sad example of the Church enforcing its will and its belief system upon others.

In Ivan's parable, the fires of the Inquisition are burning when Jesus himself steps into the scene. As Jesus walks in Seville, he is recognised by all the populace, as well as by the Inquisition. The people flock to him and he performs miracles – healing the blind and raising back to life a child from her coffin. This last act draws the attention of the Grand Inquisitor. The Grand Inquisitor is an old man of almost ninety years who, despite his age, has managed to take an active role in this latest inquisition, having burned nearly one hundred *heretics* the day before. The Grand Inquisitor orders his *holy* guard to arrest Jesus and he is led away to the dungeons.

The Grand Inquisitor then enters Jesus' cell to interrogate him and this encounter forms the centre-piece of the parable. Jesus is silent before the Inquisitor's words and merely listens. The Inquisitor commences his interrogation by mocking Jesus' silence and claiming that Jesus does not have a right to speak because to do so would encroach on people's freedom in their faith – if Jesus spoke then all would have to obey his announcements and so would not be free. This introduces the main theme of the parable – freedom and control – which links in directly to the freewill defence. The Inquisitor characterises Jesus as being concerned with promoting people's freedom whereas the Inquisition represents control. It is the Inquisitor's belief that control is better than freedom and that since Jesus' death and resurrection in the first century AD, the church has taken over the leadership of humanity from Jesus and has exercised control in this. The people have given their freedom and laid it at the feet of the church in obedience and so the Inquisitor is concerned that Jesus has come back to interfere. The church and the Inquisition "have overcome freedom, and have done so in order to make people happy".[44]

The Inquisitor then begins a discussion of the three temptations of Christ by Satan in the wilderness (Matthew 4: 1–11, Mark 1: 12–13, Luke 4: 1–13). The temptations represent challenges to Jesus' approach to his mission. If he had succumbed to the temptations, he could have effectively forced all to believe in him but, by resisting, he allowed people to have freedom. The first temptation was to turn the stones into bread. This represents Jesus' temptation to use miracles to bring about belief. By turning the stones into bread and performing other such spectacular miracles, humankind would have flocked to Jesus' side.

This first temptation furthermore represents Jesus' choice over whether to buy faith by miraculously providing for people's material needs. By not submitting to this temptation, the Inquisitor argues, Jesus has created a void that has been filled by a man-made tower of Babel which instead meets people's needs. In the story of the tower of Babel (Genesis (11: 4–9) humankind bands together to construct a large tower "that reaches to the heavens, so that we may make a name for ourselves" (Genesis 11: 4). The tower represents a challenge to God built on the accomplishments of humankind – an attempt to create a manmade alternative to God. The Inquisitor insists that by not providing materially for his people, Jesus has forced people to create the Roman Catholic Church in place of God. In doing so, instead of heavenly bread people have settled for earthly bread.

The Inquisitor continues, if Jesus had turned the stones into bread, he "would have answered the everlasting anguish of man as an individual being, and of the whole of mankind together, namely: 'before whom shall I bow down?'"[45]. People need an indisputable leader for all men to bow down to and, through miracle, Jesus could have been that figure. Such a universal figure would have ended all wars. However Jesus had rejected universal rule based on earthly bread in favour of freedom and heavenly bread. People were therefore free to reject him and indeed many would. This rejection led to immense suffering.

The next temptation discussed was for Jesus to prove that he was the son of God by throwing himself from the top of the temple so that his angels would catch him and bring him safely to earth. Again Jesus defied this temptation because he "did not want to enslave man by a miracle and thirsted for faith that is free, not miraculous"[46]. Since Jesus could foresee that humankind is weak and so, given this freedom, would rebel, the Inquisitor argues that humankind has suffered for Jesus' choice of freedom and Jesus is at fault for this. Even after accepting that some people are saved, the Inquisitor still charges Jesus with damning those that are not saved, for the sake of freedom. The church instead has made use of 'miracle, mystery and authority' to correct Jesus' mistake and to control humankind. Through this the church has taken back the terrible gift of freedom, which Jesus had given.

The third temptation discussed was for Jesus to worship Satan in exchange for power over all the nations of the world. Jesus rejected this, choosing instead to worship God alone. The Inquisitor admits that he and the church have succumbed to this temptation. The Inquisitor sees the Vatican state as representing the start of the process through which the church will rule over all the earth, "and then we shall think about the universal happiness of mankind"[47]. The Inquisitor rebukes Jesus for resisting this temptation for, had he succumbed, he could have brought 'universal union' to humankind and so healed people of their torment in lacking this. The Inquisitor sees three needs for people that Jesus could thereby have met: "someone to bow down to, someone to take over his conscience, and a means for uniting everyone"[48]. The Inquisitor's ultimate aim is to meet these needs through the church's acceptance of Satan's temptations. The flock, which was scattered because of Jesus' gift of freedom, would become united under the church – under whose yoke it would be happy. By being forced into obedience, the flock would no longer suffer for its feebleness and after death they would simply die. The Inquisitor concludes by taunting Jesus,

> Tomorrow, I repeat, you will see this obedient flock, which at my first gesture will rush to heap hot coals around your stake, at which I shall burn you for having come to interfere with us. For if anyone has ever deserved our stake, it is you. Tomorrow I shall burn you. I have spoken.[49]

After the Inquisitor has concluded, a silence follows whilst the Inquisitor waits for some time for Jesus to reply but instead Jesus is silent. Then suddenly, Jesus approaches the old man and "gently kisses him on his bloodless, ninety-year-old lips. That is the whole answer. The old man shudders."[50] The old man opens the door and urges his prisoner to leave, "Go and do not come again."[51] Jesus walks out and the kiss burns the Inquisitor's heart even as he holds to his views.

After Ivan has concluded his story, Alyosha challenges Ivan to renounce his views. Ivan responds:

"I will not renounce, and what then?
Will you renounce me for that? Will
you?" Alyosha stood up, went over to
him in silence, and gently kissed him
on the lips. "Literary theft!" Ivan
cried.[52]

## Jesus and Alyosha respond with a kiss

The response of both Jesus and Alyosha with a kiss is
profound. As an emotional action, rather than a rational,
vocal response, it is deliberately open to different
interpretations and to some extent defies explanation.
Firstly, it points to love and forgiveness being the only
response that can overwhelm attacks on faith. In this, it
implies that such accusations are in part as a result of hurts
within the accuser rather than pure reason. These hurts
require ministering to rather than arguing against, hence a
response of love, which is intended to bring healing. Also,
such a response to the arch rationalist, Ivan, undermines
his very use of reason in matters of faith. But just as
logical argument cannot defeat the kiss so the kiss cannot
defeat the argument because they do not meet each other
but instead lie on opposite sides of the ditch.
Fundamentally, the kiss is a response, not an answer.

The use of the kiss in Ivan's story and the challenge that it
represents to the Inquisitor implies some ambiguity in how
the story should be interpreted. Perhaps the most curious
aspect of this passage is in trying to decipher what exactly
Ivan's view is and whether he is wholeheartedly arguing
in favour of the Inquisitor as he seems to be. Ivan recounts
this story in the context of a rant against God and the story
is intended to further bolster his case and so we might
naturally conclude that he is in agreement with the
Inquisitor in his attacks on God. Perhaps Ivan wishes that

Jesus had actually succumbed to temptation and forced belief on humankind so that he could escape his inner torments that would eventually deteriorate into insanity. However, Ivan's choice of the Inquisition as the background and his choice of a Grand Inquisitor, who has just burned one hundred people, challenges this conclusion for the Inquisitor is hardly a sympathetic character. Alyosha himself argues with Ivan that the story praises Jesus rather than attacking him however Ivan maintains his case against faith. This ambiguity implies that Ivan is wrestling with the issue, has not yet settled the case against God and that he is muddled and tormented.

## The Inquisitor and freewill

The parable of the Grand Inquisitor is perhaps the definitive metaphor for the freewill defence in literature. Ivan presents us with a stark choice. If we side with Jesus then we are faced with a world that has freedom but also immense suffering. It is a freedom that is built on the suffering of the innocents and so it is a freedom that Ivan feels compelled to reject. This is a world where many will reject God, through sin or through unbelief, and so suffer for it. It is a world where children are allowed to suffer, sometimes horrendously. This is the world in which we live.

The alternative would be a world in which Jesus had followed the Inquisitor's advice and succumbed to Satan's temptations. This is a world without any doubts and consequently without any faith. A world where Jesus reigns through power and might and forces his benign will on all people. It is also a world without freedom to love and to hate. This is the choice that Ivan presents us with and it is a choice that we consider further in the next chapter.

God in Pain

John Henry Moule Chamberlain

# Is evil a price worth paying for the gift of freewill?

## Plantinga's summary

Alvin Plantinga, gave an excellent, technical definition of the freewill defence, with which it is useful to begin our discussion in this chapter,

> A world containing creatures who are significantly free (and freely perform more good than evil actions) is more valuable, all else being equal, than a world containing no free creatures at all. Now God can create free creatures, but He can't cause or determine them to do only what is right. For if He does so, then they aren't significantly free after all; they do not do what is right freely. To create creatures capable of *moral good*, therefore, He must create

creatures capable of moral evil; and He can't give these creatures the freedom to perform evil and at the same time prevent them from doing so. As it turned out, sadly enough, some of the free creatures God created went wrong in the exercise of their freedom; this is the source of moral evil. The fact that free creatures sometimes go wrong, however, counts neither against God's omnipotence nor against His goodness; for He could have forestalled the occurrence of evil only by removing the possibility of moral good.[53]

## But why can't we have both?

The previous chapter left us with what seemed to be an unpalatable choice – either we submit to the Grand Inquisitor, lose our freewill and become slaves or we accept a world that includes brutal, hurtful suffering. Writing this I naturally think that surely, there must be a third way – a way that we can have freewill without any of the suffering or at least without the worst of it. Is it really a foolish request? The philosopher, Julian Baggini[54] seems to think not. In one of his books, he discusses the problem of evil, and argues that if God had created us with more empathy or as better learners then we would have been less prone to hurt one another. Is this the third, better way?

There is, I believe, a flaw in this argument. The level of empathy that we feel for one another's pain is, in part, determined by how sensitive we are to our own pain. Thus a person who is regarded as insensitive to others may be doing so because they are insensitive themselves – they do not feel offended by every unkind word and so they do not expect others to feel offended either. If we all had high levels of empathy then, maybe, we would commit fewer atrocities on each other but the net level of hurt experienced could well be the same or even greater since we would all be more sensitive to it. If, on the other hand, we were all very insensitive to pain then we might commit even worse atrocities on one another with the same end result in relation to the amount of suffering that was felt.

Putting empathy to one side for a moment, is it possible that God could have made the world to contain slightly less pain without impacting on our freewill? We're not talking here about eliminating suffering altogether but rather an incremental improvement in people's lives. This is a deeply difficult question to answer and there are two prongs to it. Firstly, could God make the world slightly less painful by intervening in specific events without compromising freewill? As a believer in miracles, I believe that the answer to that is *yes*. The second prong is a more general one. This is the one that Baggini looks at – could God have set His creation up in such a way as to slightly reduce the level of pain experienced. Though I disagree with Baggini's example, I think that the answer here is probably also a *yes*. I think of the development of certain diseases, of natural disasters and of the power of the atomic bomb are aspects of creation where things could have been otherwise. Even if we see such things as being connected to the Fall of humankind from the garden of Eden, we must still accept that creation was set up in such a way as to allow disease to be an expression and consequence of the Fall.

If, on the other hand, we want to answer *no* to these questions then we are forced to believe that creation is as good as it could be, all things considered. This is the view of Leibniz and is discussed later in the chapter, *God intends all things for good?* I however do not agree with Leibniz, but I do believe that God is all-loving and all-powerful. How do I reconcile my beliefs? I believe that pain and suffering are a part of a creation that includes freewill no matter what. Arguing about whether things could be improved slightly seems to me to be evading the central question and to be merely an intellectual exercise. To put it another way, a child may wonder why her pet dog has died. The answer is in the general proposition that all dogs die and so her dog has died. The child may then wonder why her dog died today and not next week. The answer is in the specific case of her dog but it does not change the importance of the fact that her dog must die. The specific pales in significance with the general. The fact that evil exists is of paramount importance, the level of evil that exists can only ever be secondary.

### Are we clockwork oranges?

Anthony Burgess considers freewill and the problem of evil in his book, *A Clockwork Orange*. This is a title that is perhaps best known because of the notoriety of its later film adaptation. Indeed the film was withdrawn from distribution in England for 27 years as a result of some alleged copycat violence. The notoriety is a product of its subject matter, which is deliberately shocking, but it is a shame that it is the notoriety which has come to define the book rather than its profound message.

*A Clockwork Orange* tells the story of Alex, the member of a gang of so-called droogs who roam the streets of their dystopian world causing havoc as they go on their crime sprees. The depiction of their crime sprees led to the controversy since the crimes committed are brutal. The gang carry out savage acts of violence including attacking another gang; attacking members of the public; and breaking into a married couple's home where they beat the husband and raped the wife. The book is quite right in that it does not shrink from describing these acts in their full brutality. As a reader I was left feeling deeply uneasy and even angry at the injustice of the wanton destruction that these characters committed.

Having shocked the reader with this brutality, the novel turns in a different direction as Alex is arrested for murder and sent to prison. It is there that Alex agrees to be a subject in medical trials to test the effectiveness of a new medical treatment called the Ludovico technique. The technique itself is an attempt to change the way that Alex perceives and experiences violence such that instead of feeling a perverse pleasure in committing acts of violence, Alex will instead feel physically repulsed. The technique achieves this by forcing Alex to watch violent imagery on television while under the influence of drugs that cause nausea. Alex therefore develops an association in his mind between violence and nausea, which results in his new found physical repulsion to violence and ultimately his release from prison. There is however an unintended secondary consequence – whilst undergoing the Ludovico technique, classical music is played to Alex and so Alex also feels physically sick whenever he hears classical music. This is a tragedy for Alex because classical music is one of his great loves.

The concept of a Ludovico technique is a central philosophical element in the book. Under this treatment, Alex effectively has his ability to do evil through violence removed. He is no longer able to rape or to fight and so the rest of society is *better* as a result. By undergoing this treatment Alex has thereby limited his own freedom and effectively his freewill. Is society, and indeed Alex himself, better off as a result of this limitation? The unintended loss to Alex of the ability to listen to classical music is representative of his loss. Classical music is a symbol of the beauty of freedom – the very freedom that Alex has given up.

We as readers are challenged by this story. The behaviour of Alex and the droogs in the first half of the novel is truly appalling and causes immense suffering to those impacted by it. However, does this suffering justify the loss of Alex's freewill? This is the central tenet of the freewill theodicy – would living in a world of *clockwork oranges*, a world where we were all unable to sin and, through that sin, to hurt one another, would such a world be *better* than the one we have? Would we rather all be pain-free clockwork oranges, nigh on automatons, or would we prefer to have freedom and all its ugly, as well as beautiful, consequences?

### Without freedom, can I truly love? And if I love, will I then suffer?

Trying to understand the nature of freewill and its implications is deeply problematic. Some people may believe that humans do not have freewill and so our perception that we do is false. They believe that what we call *freewill* is actually us trying to make sense of our consciousness and placing the label of *freewill* on it. The existence of the debate on freewill points to the elusiveness of the subject and is a warning to be careful not to make our claims too bold when discussing the implications of a world without freedom. Would we be robots in such a world? Would we have consciousness? Would our experience of what it is to be human change in any way or would it merely continue as it is, albeit that it would present us with a false impression of reality as we mistakenly assumed that were free?

What then should we make of the assertion that true love is impossible without both parties being free? This is, I believe, a valid assertion in spite of the difficulties that may at first appear. It is surely a part of the definition of love that it is between free parties and so, if one of the parties is not free then that party cannot love. This is coupled with the viewpoint that love cannot be forced.

What then of the implications of love? According to Jürgen Moltmann, the twentieth century German theologian, love is intimately associated with suffering:

> For love leaves us open to wounding
> and disappointment. It makes us ready
> to suffer. It leads us out of isolation
> into a fellowship with others, with
> people different from ourselves, and
> this fellowship is always associated
> with suffering.[55]

This association of love and suffering rings true. For when we love another, we are open to being hurt by the other. Someone who truly does not love anyone else is, in a sense, shielded from being deeply hurt by anyone else. However, they will not be truly living, for to love is a fundamental part of human life. For those of us that do love and are loved, because we are imperfect sinners, we invariably hurt each other as we betray or disappoint one another. Nevertheless, love is worth the suffering that comes with it. If we cannot love without freewill, then is freewill is worth suffering for?

**Couldn't we be free but unable to sin?**

Charles Journet was a Swiss, Roman Catholic theologian who lived from 1891 to 1975 and was a cardinal in the Roman Catholic church. In 1961, he wrote *The Meaning of Evil*,[56] which comments on the problem of evil. In this book he raised the question of whether God could have created people so that they would be free but also unable to sin. This is slightly different to the more common question as to whether people could be free and capable of sinning but always choose not to which we discuss afterwards.

To open the discussion, Journet refers to saved people in heaven and to the angels. They have freewill but, because of the manifest and continuous vision of the Almighty before them, they never choose to sin. This vision of God does not destroy their freewill but it does enable them to overcome sin in themselves. Next Journet asks whether, since this vision has such an effect, God could have made use of it from the start and appeared before humankind so that people would never have fallen into sin. Journet answers that this would indeed have been possible. By way of illustration, such a scenario would have resulted in a Garden of Eden in which God never left the side of Adam and Eve so that, when the serpent approached, they would not have been tempted to take the apple. The lack of temptation would not have been due to Adam and Eve not wanting to be caught by God in an act of disobedience but rather it would have been as a result of the overwhelming aura of goodness and love, which God's presence would produce. However, such a world would lack the resurrection and the forgiveness brought about by Christ because there would be no Fall.

Journet goes on to argue that the immediate presence of God is effectively so overwhelming that it restricts the ability of God's creatures to make that initial free choice to love God. Effectively, if God were immediately present and apparent to all from the beginning of creation onwards then we couldn't help but choose to be with Him and so would not be truly free and could not truly choose Him – His immediate presence is irresistible. For Journet, this free choice of love is, "the most perfect flower of His paradise, to purchase which He is willing to run the risk of refusal by those of His creatures who wish to reject Him."[57]

John Hick raised a valid criticism of Journet at this point. Firstly, contrary to Journet's statement, God was not actually running a 'risk of refusal' since, before creation, He could foresee whether or not any of His creatures would freely choose Him. Furthermore, since God can foresee the outcome, He could have only created those people who would freely choose Him and not those who would reject Him. Why has God instead created a universe that includes creatures that end up rejecting Him? Though a valid objection, this is not a question for theodicy since a creature that does freely choose God will still sin before and after this choice and so will still bring evil into God's creation. Hence, even if God just created people that would choose Him, there would still be evil in the world.

For Journet the fall and sin lead to redemption and forgiveness. This is a worthwhile outcome. An innocent universe that has not fallen is inferior to a fallen universe that is later redeemed. God foresaw the fall but also intended the redemption – He therefore created a universe that would fall because He intended to redeem it. This is the sum of Journet's theodicy but it is liable to an obvious attack – where suffering is at its severest, do we, like Ivan

Karamazov, seek to hand back our tickets? Is the redemption that comes justifiable if built upon the edifice of the suffering of humanity?

## What if we were created free but only ever chose what was right?

Could God have created us free, capable of sinning, but always resisting temptation and so choosing not to sin? According to Hick, Journet did not ask this question because he regarded it as self-contradictory since free, imperfect beings will always, at some point, choose sin.[58] However others have pressed this line.

The Bible says of Jesus, "For we do not have a high priest who is unable to empathize with our weaknesses, but we have one who has been tempted in every way, just as we are—yet he did not sin." (Hebrews 4: 15). Jesus was therefore a free being and yet was without sin. Couldn't God have created us all to do likewise?

Anthony Flew was a celebrated atheist in the twentieth century who, in 2004 concluded that there was in fact a God. In his days as an atheist however he was engaged, amongst other issues, in the problem of evil. In 1955, Flew wrote an essay titled *Divine omnipotence and human freedom*[59] arguing that God could indeed have created free beings that did not do evil.

Flew began his essay by discussing the three typical arguments that are used to attack the freewill defence. Firstly, the argument that there is pain and suffering that is not caused by human beings, and so is not because of human freewill. The prime example of this is the suffering of animals that occurred either before human beings came into existence or whose suffering is not caused by human freewill. However the theist might respond to this by arguing that such suffering is instead caused by the freewill of malevolent spirits.

The second attack on the freewill defence is the unjust allocation of suffering, which seems to bear no relation to an individual's own sinfulness. This attack is discussed in the chapter *But why me?* Next comes the argument that a God who is prepared to allow such evil for the sake of freewill cannot possibly be called good. However the theist can respond by arguing that no-one knows what the ultimate sum of good and the ultimate sum of evil will be hence how can anyone judge this? Finally, attacking the soul-making defence, there is the argument that God could refine people's souls by different means, without evil, since He is the creator.

Flew is ultimately dissatisfied with these arguments as he says that, "the sceptic has apparently been forced to abandon his clear-cut knock-down refutation and to resort to arguing: that there need not have been so much and/or certain kinds of evil to get the good …Such arguments may still constitute a formidable challenge; but they do leave the believer with some freedom of manoeuvre."[60]

Flew then attempts to come up with his own, conclusive, defeat of the freewill defence by arguing that, "God might have made people so that they always in fact *freely* chose the right."[61] If such a thing were possible then the freewill defence would be defeated since this would surely be a better situation than the world that we find ourselves in. To argue for this, Flew starts by considering what it means to be 'free to choose'. He reasons that it is possible for a free action to be both predictable and caused. To illustrate this point, he gives the example of a marriage proposal. A man's decision to propose to his girlfriend can be entirely predictable to his friends as well as being entirely caused by the relationship that preceded it. Nevertheless it is still the man's free choice. The predictability of a free event could, Flew argues, therefore be predictable with 100% accuracy such that it is essentially foreknown and yet it would still be free.

Flew concludes that an action could be free as well as being foreknown and 'fully determined by caused causes'. I think however that Flew has here stretched his point too far. Let us reconsider the analogy of a man choosing to make a marriage proposal to his girlfriend. Such a man could surprise us all by freely choosing not to propose but to instead elope with his ex-girlfriend. Human beings are always capable of surprising each other and behaving in unpredictable ways and their actions are never caused to such an extent that they are fully determined and will never choose to do otherwise. Hence, I think that Flew has taken this a step too far; nevertheless, we will continue to follow Flew's argument.

Flew argues that if actions can be free, predictable and determined by causes then all free actions could be determined in advance by an all-powerful being and, this being the case, it should be possible for God to arrange "the laws of nature [such] that all men freely choose to do the right."[62] In other words, since free actions can be foreknown and determined by their cause, God could know and determine in advance what the world would become, based on how He created it. He should therefore be able to create it in such a way that there was no evil.

Next Flew looks at theodicies which state that the existence of *lower-order evils* brings out *higher-order goods*. Forgiveness is one such *higher-order good* and Flew argues that forgiveness could instead be the result of a mistaken belief in evil rather than the existence of an actual evil. In other words, we can express forgiveness to another for the perception of being sinned against, whether or not we have in truth been sinned against. Such forgiveness is a *higher-order good* and so *higher-order goods* are possible without evil. I would question here though whether forgiveness born out of the suffering caused by real evil is of the same order as forgiveness born out of a perceived, but ultimately fake, evil. Surely forgiveness, in its noblest form, is forgiveness for something suffered?

Turning to the soul-making theodicy, Flew argues that if all people always choose to do good then there would be no need for soul-making in the first place. For the end product of the soul-making process is souls that always choose good, and God could have created them in this way in the first place without the need for evil to refine them. What need therefore for evil?

J.L. Mackie was another eminent twentieth century atheist who argued along similar lines to Flew. In his essay, *Evil and Omnipotence*, published in the journal *Mind* also in 1955, he argued that if it's logically possible for a person to freely choose to do good on one occasion then it's also logically possible for all people to freely choose to do good on all occasions. Alternatively, Mackie argues, couldn't God simply override people's freewill whenever they are about to do evil?

Hick, I believe, gives a convincing response to the attacks of both Flew and Mackie by looking at the relationship between God and man, which Mackie has not addressed.

Hick argues that, "according to Christianity, the divine purpose for men is not only that they shall freely act rightly towards one another but that they shall also freely enter into a filial personal relationship with God himself."[63] Therefore it is important to ask whether God could have created people such that they would all freely respond to Him in love? Such a love would seem a hollow love in comparison to a truly free love, which must include the possibility of rejection. This free rejection of God is also known as sin and it is sin that is the cause of evil in the world. This goes back to the point I made earlier whether without freewill, we can truly love.

A further, compelling response to these attacks is given by Stephen T. Davis who approaches it from a different angle. Davis argues that it is logically possible for free beings to always freely choose the good although it is highly improbable. However, were this to happen, "it would have been a pleasant accident. God would not have brought it about, nor would God be responsible for it. For if the agents were really free, no-one could have caused them to behave as they did."[64] This is the key point – if humans are free, then they have to be able to choose to sin; there must be that possibility. Hence, how can God pre-determine that they do otherwise?

**A discussion with a friend**
I had an interesting debate about freewill and morality with a good friend of mine whilst I was working on this book. We were approaching the subject from different viewpoints since my friend is an atheist. Not being philosophers, we were not concerned with exactly the same issues as that of Flew and Mackie, however, like them, our discussion became concerned with whether it would have been possible for God to create humans such

that they would always choose the morally perfect thing since we both viewed this as being at the heart of the freewill defence.

Having agreed that God would not have created humanity perfect, we hit upon the question of whether to be free and to always choose the good (the morally perfect thing), humanity would have to be perfect in every way or just morally perfect. I argued that morality is so intrinsic to the nature of a creature that the creature would have to be perfect in most ways in order to achieve moral perfection. My argument was that a human's morality is not a quality that can be separately changed. For example, God could not take me as I am and then adjust me so that I became morally perfect but was otherwise identical to how I had been previously. For God to make me morally perfect, and I am not being falsely modest here, He would have to change me utterly – my emotions, my sensitivity, my ambitions and drive, my kindness and my lovingness – such that I would be an almost completely different person. The creature that I became, where kindness and lovingness were created qualities rather than choices, would also surely lack freewill? Morality, and always choosing the good, is not therefore the same as hair colour that can be easily adjusted, rather it is an outworking of one's whole being.

My friend proposed the counter argument that being morally perfect is just one characteristic among many and although many characteristics are linked, morality is not so intrinsic to a being that it necessitates complete perfection in the being. Rather it is a state of mind and therefore someone doesn't have to be entirely perfect in order to be morally perfect. Since God can create people as morally imperfect, he should also be able to create them as morally perfect. The difficulty of the task here is not an issue for God, rather the issue is whether it is possible.

### And what does our freedom say about God?

The freewill defence rests on the assumption that we do live in a world with freewill – where we are able to exercise our free choices and choose to do either good or evil. Not all Christian theologians would agree with this argument – some would instead see a more deterministic universe that is tightly controlled by God. With God determining all, they naturally depend upon the soul-making defence as their explanation for evil.

If freewill is indeed real then this says something about God. By giving humankind freewill, God has limited himself in some respects. If we now have freewill, God has to respect that by allowing us to exercise it. He cannot arbitrarily intervene to restrict and confine our freewill and He is therefore limited in not being able to do so. For whenever God makes a decision, He limits Himself by not being able to decide the opposite. Going back to the central tension of the problem of evil – the existence of a good, all-powerful God and the existence of evil – the freewill defence eases this tension by restricting God's power. By creating free beings, God is, in a sense, no longer all-powerful.

André LaCocque reflects on this,

> [God's] omnipotence is a pre-creational fact. Paradoxically, with the creation act God uses His power to limit His omnipotence and omniscience, which would leave no room whatsoever to another being

beside Him. Once there is creation, there is self-limitation of the Creator, for He chooses to have a partner to fulfil with Him the total excellence of creation continua ...No one and nothing in God's universe is robotised[65]

## Do we actually have freewill?

This seems a strange question to ask since we all experience life under the impression that we are free agents and that we determine our own choices. However it is a necessary question since it is an important logical step in establishing the validity of the freewill defence.

For many years after the Enlightenment, the deterministic view was popular amongst scientists. This view was linked to Newtonian physics, which can be interpreted as saying that the outcome of a physical event can be predicted when all factors are known. It was just a short leap from that to the view that, likewise, all human actions can be predicted since, according to such thinkers, humans are just physical. This view was to take a knock from the discoveries of quantum physics in the twentieth century when observations of the interactions of particles at the sub-atomic level consistently showed results that were inherently unpredictable such that the same experiment could be repeated many times with different outcomes. These observations challenged the deterministic thinkers however they did not prove freewill, rather the more troubling conclusion of randomness.

Within Christianity itself, perhaps the thinker most often associated with determinism was John Calvin, the reformation theologian who lived from 1509 to 1564. Calvin's view of predestination implies a more deterministic universe where God chooses who is saved and who is not saved. In Calvin's theology, God is much more in control of the course of history. It therefore appears difficult to hold the freewill defence and Calvinism together.

Predestinarian verses in the Bible such as Ephesians 1: 11, Philippians 2: 12–13 and Romans 9: 6–29 do indeed present theological difficulties to the reader and many different interpretations of them have been developed over the years. However they do not, in my opinion, refer to freewill itself but rather to God's choice and grace in the salvation of His people. Viewing these verses in a dualist framework with freewill at one end and determinism at the other is not therefore appropriate. For example, Philippians 2: 12–13 states,

> Therefore, my dear friends, as you have always obeyed—not only in my presence, but now much more in my absence—continue to work out your salvation with fear and trembling, for it is God who works in you to will and to act in order to fulfil His good purpose.

These two verses, taken at face value imply both freewill as well as determinism. Firstly, both Paul's exaltation to the reader to "continue to work out" and his reference to his friends' obedience imply that the friends have a choice in the matter, that it is the friends' works that he is referring to – hence freewill. Indeed, all of the instructions and commandments given in the Bible must first presume that the readers have freewill. Complementarily, Paul's reference in Philippians to "God works in you to will and to act..." implies a partnership with God that can be interpreted as being on the side of determinism. The presence of both these aspects in close proximity implies a cohesion between the two. To conclude from these verses that we do not have freewill at all requires that we ignore the first part and so cannot be an adequate conclusion.

As part of our own human experience, we all experience something that we describe as freewill. We feel responsible for our own actions, hence guilt, and we expect others to feel responsible for theirs. When we choose to do something, we experience it as a free choice. The question at hand therefore is whether this perception of freedom is in fact an illusion. Are our senses deceiving us? To argue that the universe is deterministic is therefore to argue against our senses. This is a debate that will perhaps never be settled but my instinct is to trust my own experience such that what I do experience as freedom is not a figment of my imagination but is in fact free.

God in Pain

# God intends all things for good?

I think I first heard it preached that God intends all things for good when I was a teenager. The belief that this sermon proposed was along the lines that everything is in God's plan and is according to His purpose and so everything will work out for the best. As a response to theodicy, this essentially denies the evilness of evil for if everything, even the apparently evil events in the world, works out for the best then ultimately they must be good even though there may be some present suffering.

Various stories have been used to justify this view, such as the story that I once heard of how Christianity came to Korea. Robert Jermain Thomas was a protestant missionary who developed a heart to bring the gospel to the Korean people and first visited Korean in 1865. However his work as a missionary was to be tragically cut short as he was killed, just a year later, in 1866 whilst in Korea. This was not the end of the story though for his murderer is said to have taken Robert's Bibles and used their pages to wallpaper his house. Over the years, people read this wallpaper and gradually became convinced of the truth of the gospel and so, through this man's sacrifice, the gospel was spread as people came from far and wide to read the words on the wall. Eventually this led to a church being established in the area. Hence, God redeemed the tragedy of his death. This is an inspiring story – Robert Jermain Thomas' sacrifice should rightly give us all hope that our actions may not be in vain. Nevertheless, this is not the universal model for much suffering is without any obvious redemption.

## Psalms 22 and 23 and triumphalist Christianity

Whilst at university, I attended a Christian Union. It was a place of faith in the storms that many experience at university. However, they once opened a meeting with a drama that purported to show the impact of conversion to Christianity on the main character. The character told how, before she was a Christian, her life was meaningless and unhappy but having become a Christian, her life became meaningful and happy. What contrived nonsense I thought as I watched. The purpose of knowing God has never been about being happy, or being removed from the suffering of the world. As George MacDonald said, "The Son of God suffered unto the death, not that men might not suffer, but that their sufferings might be like His"[66]. There are countless verses in the Bible that testify to the suffering of God's people – for example, the so called *dark psalms* that express the pain and suffering of the Christian life; the sufferings of the Israelites in Egypt; and the references of Paul to his 'present sufferings'.

I think that there has developed, within some streams of modern Christianity, a view that suffering and particularly emotional suffering, is linked to sin or to spiritual immaturity. The Christian who is depressed is somehow lacking in their faith or struggling with sin. Physical suffering is generally viewed differently. Perhaps this is because the Bible points out the error of this when Jesus heals the sick, for example in John (9: 1–3), "As he went along, he saw a man blind from birth. His disciples asked him, 'Rabbi, who sinned, this man or his parents, that he was born blind?' 'Neither this man nor his parents sinned,' said Jesus, 'but this happened so that the work of God might be displayed in his life'". However, for some Christians, emotional suffering is viewed as showing, at the least, a lack of faith, and at worst, sin. I would love for people who have such views to meet King David, the writer of many of the psalms. David was a man who loved God, his psalms reflected his dedication to and love of God. Psalm 23 is a good example of this:

> The Lord is my shepherd, I lack nothing.
> He makes me lie down in green pastures,
> He leads me beside quiet waters,
> He refreshes my soul.
> He guides me along the right paths
> for His name's sake.
> Even though I walk
> through the darkest valley,
> I will fear no evil,
> for You are with me;
> Your rod and Your staff,
> they comfort me.
> You prepare a table before me
> in the presence of my enemies.
> You anoint my head with oil;

> my cup overflows.
> Surely your goodness and love will
> follow me
> all the days of my life,
> and I will dwell in the house of the Lord
> forever.

And yet psalm 22, which precedes this, famously begins with the words, "My God, my God, why have you forsaken me?" The words that Jesus would use on the cross to express his desperation and sense of abandonment by God. Two consecutive psalms, two very different responses to suffering.

The Bible is a profound book, it speaks with many voices but with one message. I see this as a part of the beauty of it, the Bible holds in tension the sense of rejection by God that we can feel alongside the triumphal sense of the love of God that we can also feel. To emphasise one aspect over the other will surely diminish the message. We must instead dwell in this tension when we read the Bible and dwell in the confusion between the two. The Lord is our shepherd and yet at times He seems to abandon us.

### Jeremiah

Probably the most famous verse in Jeremiah is in chapter 29, where verse 11 says, "'For I know the plans I have for you,' declares the Lord, 'plans to prosper you and not to harm you, plans to give you hope and a future.'" This is a verse often quite rightly used by those who wish to give hope to others, for our God does indeed love us. However, there are times when He allows us to go through suffering.

Based solely on my knowledge of this verse, when I read Jeremiah I expected to find a book full of hope and encouragement. I couldn't have been further from the truth. For, the book of Jeremiah actually focuses on God's judgement. This is why I find it remarkable that the most famous verse in Jeremiah is the one above, a verse that does not at all reflect the tone of the book. It is quite natural that each generation of Christians places emphasis on different aspects of their faith. For example, in the day of Jonathan Edwards, the eighteenth century American preacher, the emphasis was more on fire and brimstone, judgement and repentance. The modern, evangelical church has instead placed emphasis on grace, forgiveness and loving relationship with God. It seems that God is too big for one generation to fully grasp and so we can only draw upon aspects of Him, but there is surely something wrong going on here?

## Our present sufferings

It always feels like an inadequate response to refer to the rewards of heaven when discussing suffering. We are suffering now, whilst heaven is in the future, so how does that help us here and now? But of course it is in fact an entirely appropriate and Biblical response to the problems that we experience now; for the hope of the life to come can cheer us in times of suffering.

The apostle Paul experienced great suffering in his own life principally through persecution. Having been taught the Bible stories at Sunday school, it is easy to have a romanticised view of the persecution experienced by the early church with those persecuted seen as heroic martyrs who suffered in joyful silence. Whilst there was a great deal of heroism in the face of such suffering, make no mistake, the persecution was brutal and bloody. In one of his letters to the Corinthian church, Paul details his own sufferings including beatings, stonings, hunger and thirst

God in Pain

(2 Corinthians 11: 23–29). Paul would of course ultimately be killed for his faith. So when Paul says, "I consider that our present sufferings are not worth comparing with the glory that will be revealed in us" (Romans 8: 18), he is not trying to sugar-coat some minor tragedy.

We must always remember therefore to see our present sufferings in their true context – the context of eternity. For all that we experience now is fleeting in comparison to heaven. Our hope in the resurrection therefore should help us in times of trouble. As C.S. Lewis remarked, "a book on suffering which says nothing of heaven, is leaving out almost the whole of one side of the account. Scripture and tradition habitually put the joys of heaven into the scale against the sufferings of earth, and no solution of the problem of pain which does not do so can be called a Christian one"[67].

There is however still one sense in which the hope of heaven does not answer the question of suffering in the here and now. Even though the suffering that we experience now may be insignificant in comparison to the glory to come, this does not explain why there is suffering in the present in the first place. The most poignant statement of this inadequacy is in the form of those people who will not go to heaven and who have no hope to comfort them since they will not have future glory. Although heaven is a comfort to some, it is not an explanation of why there is suffering now.

**Voltaire and Leibniz do battle**
In 1759 Voltaire, the French Enlightenment philosopher, wrote the book *Candide, or Optimism*. In it, he parodied another philosopher – Leibniz, whose view was that the

world in which we live is the best possible world. Leibniz had argued this in relation to the problem of evil. Leibniz was therefore arguing not that the world was perfect and without evil, but rather that the world was the best that it could possibly be. Were such a thing to be proved it would resolve the problem of evil. However, as has often been pointed out, Leibniz lived a comparatively comfortable life compared to many in his age and this may have influenced his thinking. Leibniz was relatively wealthy and so further removed from some of the tragedy of the day-to-day existence of the time. For Leibniz, theodicy was a purely theoretical issue.

Voltaire's book, a mocking critique of Leibniz's idea, tells the story of a young man named Candide who wanders from one human tragedy to the next – from rape, to murder, to near execution and earthquake. However, since Candide believes in *Optimism* – Leibniz's theory that we live in the best possible world – he begins with a cheery outlook on life despite his plight. In order to defend his view, Candide tries to explain the suffering he sees and how it must all be for the good. Gradually the character of Candide develops over the course of the novel as he begins to question this theodicy because of the events that he witnesses. At the start, on seeing suffering, he defends Optimism to his cynical companion, Martin:

> 'I have seen worse,' Candide replied.
> 'But a wise man, who has since had
> the misfortune to be hanged, taught
> me that there is in these things a
> perfect propriety; like the shadows in
> a beautiful painting.' – 'Your hanged
> man was making a mockery of us,'
> interjected Martin, 'and your shadows

> are in truth dreadful stains.' – 'It is
> men who make these stains,' said
> Candide, 'and they cannot do
> otherwise.' – 'So it is not their fault,
> then,' said Martin."[68]

Like Dostoevsky and his stories of suffering, Voltaire is keen to root his novel in real life events for that is crucial to his argument with Leibniz. The earthquake that Candide witnesses is the famous Lisbon earthquake. Later in the novel, on witnessing the suffering of a slave, Candide is asked by his companion, 'What is Optimism?', and his response reveals his new found disillusionment with Leibniz's ideas, "it is the mania for insisting that all is well when all is by no means well"[69]. The initial naivety of Candide's view of suffering is the ultimate undoing of his belief in the best of all possible worlds. To compare some of the horrific scenes that he observes to shadows in a painting that increase the beauty of the painting is an appalling statement to make and Martin is right to rebuke Candide for this.

Sometimes, as Christians, we behave like Candide. We talk of our blessings and our struggles and develop a positive narrative to describe our lives in the context of a loving God and His plans for us which bears no relation to the truth. This approach to life can fail when it does not acknowledge the possibility for painful defeat and suffering. Yes, we should see our lives in the context of our loving Father but we must not do so in a way that doesn't allow for failure, suffering and times in the wilderness. For if we do then we will be like Candide at the start of the novel – ignorant and in denial of the truth of life on this earth. This will make us susceptible to losing our faith the first time that we encounter real tragedy. If our theodicies do not allow for unjustifiable, painful suffering, then we too will surely become disillusioned. Likewise, we must be cautious in our counselling of others not to diminish their suffering by comparing it to shadows, or other inappropriate metaphors, as we seek to justify a bankrupt theodicy.

## Soul-making and universalism

The *best of all possible worlds* defence is a trap into which proponents of the soul-making defence sometimes stumble as they seek to minimise the impact of evil in their arguments. There is another related trap that impacts this defence and it is that of universalism – that everyone is saved. It is interesting to note that John Hick, a modern proponent of the soul-making defence, is a universalist.[70] It is my view that universalism is a natural consequence of adopting the soul-making defence. For, under this theodicy, the purpose of the evil in the world is to improve the souls of humanity as part of the process of redeeming those souls. If we adopt this view then unredeemed souls present a problem. They surely do not derive any benefit from suffering since they are unredeemed at the end and so any improvement in their souls has not brought about their salvation. Their suffering may help to develop the souls of those that are redeemed but this presents us with a gross injustice – why should they suffer for the sake of other's souls? Universalism may be the only answer to this question.

## A stumbling block

The verse in the book of Romans, "And we know that in all things God works for the good of those who love Him, who have been called according to His purpose" (Romans 8: 28) has always been a stumbling block to me. How then do I make sense of it in the face of the suffering that I witness – suffering that often appears to have no redemptive purpose but is another of Voltaire's stains. Were it not for the word "all" it might not be so difficult but I believe that the Bible is true in its totality and so I cannot ignore this one word or this verse.

Henri Blocher's view may be relevant here. When he discusses God's work in the life of Joseph in the book of Genesis,[71] Blocher argues against the view that God turned the evil in Joseph's betrayal by his brothers into good. Rather Blocher argues that God corrects the evil of the situation by intervening and so brings about a good outcome. It seems a subtle distinction but is actually fundamental to our understanding of suffering for it shows that evil is not good but that its consequences can be transformed to bring about good.

Reconciling a reading of Romans with reading some of the protest at suffering that occurs in the Old Testament is difficult and this difficulty hints that maybe a face-value reading of Romans is not satisfactory. I hope however that I am not guilty of seeking to neutralise Romans 8: 28 to favour my own theological standpoint. For me, the key to interpreting the verse is its context. Paul writes these words whilst discussing future glory. A few sentences earlier he has written, "I consider that our present sufferings are not worth comparing with the glory that will be revealed in us." (Romans 8: 18) and so he is here focused on heaven and the future. It is in this context that God uses "all things", for in the fullness of eternity, God can use "all things" to work for good. This does not mean that He directly causes each and every thing or intends them all, merely that He can and will redeem all our sufferings in the glory that is to come. It is comforting to know this and it is not a challenge to the evilness of evil or a denial of the need to cry out whilst suffering. Rather it is a promise of a glorious future. If we do not perceive this redemption in our lifetimes, we can know that it will happen in the future that is to come.

God in Pain

# The problem of good

**The problem of good – an atheist's dilemma**

The problem of evil has a mirror image that must also be considered – that of the problem of good. C.F.D. Moule, a leading New Testament scholar and a relative of mine in the Moule family, once wrote that, "goodness that springs up in the middle of evil has got to be accounted for; and if we're honest, we have to admit that this presents a serious problem. Where does it come from? What is its source?"[72] . As N.T. Wright, another New Testament scholar, elaborated,

> Even if you're an atheist, you face the problem [of evil] the other way up: is this world a sick joke, which contains some things which make us think it's a wonderful place, and other things which make us think it's an awful place, or what? ...if the world is the

> chance assembly of accidental phenomena, why is there so much that we want to praise and celebrate? Why is there beauty, love and laughter?[73]

Harry Emerson Fosdick also states the problem of good well after having first considered the problem of evil,

> Once I decided that I could not believe in the goodness of God in the presence of the world's evil, and then I discovered that I had run headlong into another and even more difficult problem: What to do about all the world's goodness on the basis of no God? Sunsets and symphonies, mothers, music and the laughter of children at play, great books, great art, great science, great personalities, victories of goodness over evil, the long hard-won ascent from the Stone Age up, and all the friendly spirits that are to other souls a 'cup of strength in some great agony' – how can we, thinking of these on the basis of no God, explain them as the casual accidental by-products of physical forces, going it blind? I think it cannot be done. The mystery of evil is very great upon the basis of a good God but the mystery of goodness is impossible upon the basis of no God.[74]

This argument strikes me as profound and it merits further discussion. If there is something that we perceive to be goodness in this universe then it has to be explained. The Christian can offer the explanation that a good and loving God is its source but I am not sure what explanation an atheist could provide. Hick argues that, "the atheist is not obliged to explain the universe at all. He can simply accept it at its face value as an enormously complex natural fact"[75] but I am far from convinced by this. Surely the atheist scientist would not be satisfied with an unexplained universe but would seek to explain the universe within the framework of their atheism? I offer the thoughts that follow by way of reflection on the matter rather than as anything that could be seen as an argument for the existence of God.

### A thought experiment

In a similar vein to Philo's thought experiment raised by Hume and described in Appendix I, I would like to propose an alternative thought experiment. Whereas Philo's thought experiment asked what a universe created by a good God would look like, mine will approach the subject from the opposite angle. Let us try to imagine what a godless universe might look like. Or to phrase the question differently, what might be the characteristics common to universes in which there was no God?

It strikes me that a godless universe would not necessarily have life in it in the first place. It might well be formless and void – ruled by chaotic forces that were insensitive to the possibility of life. Or perhaps it would have no rules at all – the laws of physics would alter every second resulting in extreme unpredictability. The principal of entropy, that all things descend into chaos, would reign supreme.

The *multiverse theory* states that there exist a near infinite number of universes and that we are in one of them. Some have life and others do not; some are chaotic and others are not; and some are predictable whilst others are not. As observers it is natural that we find ourselves in a universe with life and order since observers would not be able to live in a universe without life and order. The theory therefore invents a multitude of universes in order to explain the one that we live in. We find ourselves in a universe that allows for life since we are alive. Correspondingly, according to my thought experiment, we also find ourselves in one of a range of universes that, by allowing for life, also allows for God's existence.

Another way in which a godless universe might differ is in relation to goodness and morality. Why do we find slavery and murder so abhorrent? Why do we have a sense of moral outrage at atrocities? Surely we should just seek to serve our own, and perhaps our kin's interest. Instead, whether we believe in God or not, we all seem to have a sense of right and wrong. Where does this sense of right and wrong come from and is it logical? Today's *New Atheist* will often at this juncture make the mocking observation that they don't need an ancient book to tell them right from wrong but it seems to me that they are missing the point. For the believer, right and wrong is made possible by the existence of an infinite God against which morality can be measured as a universal yardstick. The atheist instead has to rely on the basis of our common humanity as a yardstick for morality. Both though have a sense of morality and it is this morality that is compatible with the existence of a good God. We do not seek merely to behave selfishly but we seek to behave morally whether or not it is beneficial to us.

The reason that I am discussing this in the thought experiment is because in a created universe I would expect to see a belief in right and wrong. This belief in morality, in an absolute morality, has resulted in the laws against murder, robbery, rape and slavery. It has resulted in the human rights movement. Without an absolute morality, none of these things make sense. Furthermore, the belief in absolute morality is a moderating influence in almost everyone's lives. In my thought experiment, this inherent belief in morality is also consistent with the existence of God.

Finally, the problem of evil itself: the fact that we view evil as a problem, that we question God for it and feel justified in doing so, is consistent with a universe in which God exists since it points to a belief in a justice that is higher than what we perceive with our senses. Ironically, I am arguing therefore that people living in a universe that was uncreated would have no reason to question why there was evil as they would have no concept of evil.

### Altruism

The existence of altruism is hotly debated. Is it possible to be truly altruistic or are we all just driven by our selfish desires and/or genes? Some atheists would argue that we are driven by our selfish genes to serve our own self-interest. We are incapable of selfless acts since even the most seemingly selfless act is actually done to increase our own sense of pleasure. For example, if someone gives money to charity, they do so because they are following their principles and by living a life in accordance with their principles they are increasing their own pleasure.

Apart from being a deeply depressing world view I simply think that it doesn't square up to the reality of the world around us. The death of Jesus on the cross is the Christian response to such views – a truly selfless act. Furthermore there are countless examples of other people who have given their lives, both figuratively and literally, for the sake of others. It is not naive to believe in acts of heroism and altruism; it is in fact cynical to the point of naivety to believe that they don't happen.

To give one such example, a friend once recounted the following story to me in relation to his parents' divorce. He was twelve years old at the time and he and his siblings had been living with their mother. Each month she would take them to visit their father. The mother was someone who was prone to being late and on this occasion she was over an hour late when she dropped off her children. Since the father was only allowed to see his children once a month, he was naturally angry about this and so, when the mother and children arrived, the parents had a fierce row. The father was shouting and swearing at the mother. Now the reason she had been so late this time was entirely her own fault and her children had in fact been waiting for her for some time before they set off that morning. However, when my friend saw his father shouting and his mother upset, he decided to act. He said to his father that it was entirely his fault that they were late and so his father proceeded to turn his anger on his son.

Now the point of this story is that the son gained nothing from this, other than to help his mother – the benefit of which to him was negligible in terms of pleasure in comparison to the hurt from suffering his father's wrath. I do not believe that stories such as this are at all uncommon – they happen every day as people seek earnestly to do what is right. We are left still with the problem of good – we must explain where these acts come from.

**Is being good caused by evolution?**

The book, *Survival of the Nicest. How Altruism Made Us Human and Why It Pays to Get Along* by Stefan Klein also looks at the compatibility of altruism with the theory of evolution. In doing so, the accepted dogma that Klein is trying to counter is demonstrated by the words of Richard Dawkins in his book, *The Selfish Gene*. Klein summarises it by quoting from this book, "We are survival machines – robot vehicles blindly programmed to preserve the selfish molecules known as genes. ...like successful Chicago gangsters our genes have survived ...in a highly competitive world ...this gene selfishness will usually give rise to selfishness in individual behaviour."[76]

Klein's central premise is that a society that includes a portion of people that act altruistically will prosper over and above one where everyone behaves selfishly. In a world where only the fittest survive, Klein argues that there is actually an evolutionary benefit for a selfless gene and this is the cause of the selfless acts that we see. Klein uses a wealth of research to back up his claim, most of which is used to show that when humans co-operate they tend to do better economically than when they don't. One such example of this arises in the work of the mathematician John Nash, whose life was portrayed in the 2001 film, *A Beautiful Mind*. Game Theory was a standard theory at the time, which saw life as being like a game of chess with all players seeking to *win* at the expense of their opponents. Hence, people would act selfishly to win this game. It was John Nash's contribution to show that Game Theory needed refining since he argued that acting in co-operation with others, rather than in opposition to them, would often result in a more beneficial outcome for those concerned.

In my own opinion, there is a central flaw in the arguments contained in Klein's book. Contrary to the implication of the title, he assumes that people in fact only ever act in accordance with their own calculated self-interest. If people calculate that behaving altruistically will, in the long run, pay off then they will behave as such. For example, the arguments of Nash, at least as they are portrayed by Klein, assume that people will always act out of selfishness and their co-operation is only due to a desire to improve their own circumstances overall rather than purely to benefit their companions at their own expense. Klein's arguments therefore seem to assume that true altruism does not exist since true altruism is behaving in such a way that disadvantages oneself for the benefit of others and is *without reward*. Klein's form of altruism is merely a sophisticated form of selfishness. The flaw with this is that when people behave altruistically their conscious motivations are truly altruistic rather than selfish. People who risk their own lives to save a drowning person, do so because it is *right*; people give to charity because it is *just*; people help their neighbours out of compassion – not self-interest.

Despite his valiant attempt to prove otherwise, I think that Klein has therefore only confirmed the seeming contradiction between true altruism and evolution. Rather than proving that evolution and altruism work together he has instead only proved the rather less grand proposition – that evolution and selfish co-operation do so. Where then does altruism come from?

## Why does no major religion teach that God is evil?
At the risk of entering a circular argument, I think that there may be something in the fact that no major religion teaches that its most powerful god is evil. The atheist view

is that religion is created by man whilst the theist views religions, other than their own, as being man-made. Hence, for both, some or all religions will have a human element that shapes them. This human element will surely result from people trying to make sense of their environment since one of religion's roles is to make sense of the world. A world that was full of meaningless suffering with no redeeming features would therefore give rise to religions that reflected this – religions where the most powerful god was evil. On the other hand, a world without suffering, a perfect world – if such a thing were possible – would give rise to religions where the main god was entirely good and there were no dissenting spirits.

When we look at our own world and the religions that inhabit it, what do we find? No religion believes in a supreme God that is evil, rather there are elements of good and evil in all religions. In some religions evil is represented by lesser deities whilst in others it is in the form of a satanic figure. The balance of good and evil that we find in our religions implies that the universe is perceived by humanity to be fundamentally good but that there are areas of resistance to this goodness.

Therefore, if, as shown by the choices of religion, humankind perceives the world to be fundamentally good but with areas of evil then we are perhaps thrown back to the problem of goodness – where does this apparent fundamental goodness come from?

God in Pain

John Henry Moule Chamberlain

# But why me?

**Theology meets the here and now**
The particle accelerator at CERN functions by
accelerating sub atomic particles to speeds approaching
the speed of light and then smashing them into one
another. It is from these collisions that physicists are able
to identify some of the characteristics of the particles and
even discover new ones that have been flung out by the
collision as debris. When theodicy is put into practice, into
personal situations, we have the theological equivalent of
such collisions. The ideas and intellectual responses to
theodicy can only ever be truly tested when they collide
with actual suffering.

All these words that have been written by different writers
– do they help at all? Did writing *The Problem of Pain*
help C.S. Lewis when he later suffered loss? And when
suffering happens to us, when the words should become
practical, do they help us? However good a general theory

of suffering is, it is extremely difficult to apply it to a specific circumstance. 'Your father was murdered because it's important that the freewill of the murderer was maintained'. 'You're dying painfully because it will improve your soul'. Such words are far easier to apply in abstract, general ways than they are to apply to specific circumstances. So how should we proceed? Is it even right to seek to justify specific occurrences of suffering?

Many writers on theodicy have noted the uneven spread of suffering amongst people. Many of us suffer extremely in comparison to others who seem to live relatively comfortable and content lives. Indeed it is probably this unevenness, and its apparent injustice, which leads many to question the problem of evil and makes it a problem in the first place. If suffering was distributed unevenly, but in a just fashion, then Job would not have complained. Alternatively if suffering was spread evenly, we might not complain so or at least our complaints would be different. It is the injustice in the distribution of suffering that raises the starkest questions that people ask of God. Hick is among those to comment on this, "the problem consists rather in the fact that instead of serving a constructive purpose pain and misery seem to be distributed in random and meaningless ways, with the result that suffering is often undeserved and often falls upon men in amounts exceeding anything that could be rationally intended".[77]

It is this unevenness that presents particular difficulty for the soul-making defence. Are we driven by the unevenness to the perverse conclusion that those who suffer most have souls that need the most work? However, such a horrendous view would stem from a misunderstanding of the soul-making defence. Hick rejects this view[78] and argues rather that it is the existence of evil *in general* that leads to our soul-making. Hence, specific incidences of evil do not necessarily lead to our spiritual betterment but rather the existence of evil in the world in general betters us. In fact, under both the soul-making and the freewill defences, we do not need to explain all occurrences of evil as if they were all for the good of our souls or to enable us to be free. Rather the defences are concerned with understanding evil *in general*. Stephen T. Davis agrees with Hick when he argues that, "a general answer to the theodicy problem, if successful, will suffice"[79] and so we do not need to explain specific events but merely to trust God for, "ultimately, it comes down to trust".[80] Whilst I am tempted by Hick and Davis' argument, I feel that it is lacking. For specific events do matter and their view seems to diminish the importance of the specific events as well as the need for the specific victims to be heard.

Perhaps it is best to adopt a different approach and move away from the academic world of Hick and Davis. In the pastoral world, it is undeniably natural and good that we try to make sense of the events of our lives; that we question why certain things happen to us. But how can we do this when our theodicies only explain evil in general and not the specific evil events that we witness in our lives? Perhaps making sense of such events can only be found through contemplation, prayer, and ultimately revelation from God. Roger Forster made the same point, "Ultimately, however erudite our theology, we each individually need God's direct revelation to make sense of our lives and bring comfort to us in our suffering".[81]

**Unevenness compounded**
A further issue is raised if we believe in an interventionist God. This undoubtedly makes the unjust distribution of

suffering harder to understand for if God intervenes at certain times through miracles and answers to prayer then why does He not intervene at other times? The interventionist God, which I believe in, seems to compound the injustice of suffering since He has a hand in preventing some evils but not others and so is part of the cause of the imbalance. This is a frightening concept to face.

## Cosmic forces

Greg Boyd and Roger Forster, both pastors and theologians, put the uneven distribution of evil in the world down to one source – satanic forces, which are engaged in a cosmic war. As Forster says,

> Sadly people get hit indiscriminately with the shrapnel of attacks... The war in which we are engaged is as messy and as complicated as the universe in which we live. There is a randomness to the cosmic battle that Satan is waging against God ...In part, it is random because Satan and his forces are not omnipresent – they cannot be everywhere at once.[82]

Boyd and Forster's arguments have similarities, in many ways, to the theodicy expounded by David Ray Griffin in Stephen T. Davis' book, *Encountering Evil. Live Options in Theodicy*.[83] In this, Griffin argues that the world was not created out of nothing (*ex nihilo*) as is traditionally thought in Christian theology. Rather, the world was created out of a primordial chaos. This view is based on a different interpretation of Genesis (1: 1–2). Griffin then argues that, "Creation out of chaos suggests that the 'material' from which our world was created had some power of its own, so that it would not be wholly subject to the divine will."[84] Thus, like Boyd and Forster, Griffin's theodicy argues that evil is explained by the existence of a competing power to God that is unevenly spread.

## Bad things happen to good people

Whether Satanic forces or other reasons are to blame for the suffering that we experience in life, we must always heed the lesson of the book of Job – that bad things do happen to good people. With prayerful reflection, maybe we can find meaning in our suffering. Maybe on the other hand the suffering was truly meaningless and so no more than an ordeal that must be borne, whether as a result of cosmic forces or otherwise. But where does that leave us?

God in Pain

# Is it ever alright to get angry with God?

**God on trial**

There is a story that in Auschwitz a group of Jews put God on trial[85]. In the epicentre of the holocaust, they felt abandoned by God and so they charged Him with betrayal under the terms of the Jewish people's covenant with Him – a covenant that they thought would protect them from such horrors. After much discussion, which was framed in the manner of a legal trial, they eventually found Him guilty under the terms of this covenant and presumably sentenced Him to death. Having concluded the trial, the Rabbi announced that it was time for evening prayers.

Elie Wiesel witnessed this trial as a child and chose to portray a fictionalised version of it in his play *The Trial of God*. The play is not set in Auschwitz but in circumstances similar to it – a Ukrainian village in 1649 during the aftermath of a Jewish pogrom in which many Jews had been slaughtered. A Jewish innkeeper, Berish, and his daughter, Hannah, have survived the pogrom and are holed up in Berish's inn. They are joined by some travelling Jewish actors and Berish demands that they stage a trial of God rather than a more typical play. Berish takes the role of the prosecution. Sam, a satanic stranger, takes the role of the counsel for the defence.

As with Job's friends, this satanic figure uses theological academic arguments that appear to be sound. Berish's arguments on the other hand are emotional. As Matthew Fox writes in his afterword to a recent edition:

> Satan sounds oh so theologically correct and logical. He could get a job in most academic theological institutions today. Beware of theologians and excessive rationalisations, Wiesel is warning. Rightly so. For theology too easily strays into the lap of the left brain, too far from the guts where injustice as well as compassion are felt and where wonder and amazement are tasted.[86]

Berish repeatedly accuses God of being among the killers rather than with the victims. Thus Berish goes further than just saying that the atrocities of the pogrom are within God's plan, he instead argues that, by taking the side of the killers, God is not good and he accuses God of intending this evil and suffering. It is left to Satan, in the form of Sam, to correct Berish, "When human beings kill one another, where is God to be found? You see Him among the killers. I find Him among the victims."[87] Berish rejects the argument that God is among the victims for victims are powerless but God is all-powerful. Wiesel has here identified a key aspect of the problem of evil – whose side is God on? A God that is all-powerful and that directs the course of human history could be accused of being on the side of the killers for He, at the very least, gave them room to operate and so allowed their crimes to be committed. But can it really be argued that God is instead on the side of the victims – the powerless – and those who protest on their behalf?

Towards the start of the *Arab Spring*, which began in December 2010, as protests swept the Arab world, there is a related story that I heard that struck a chord with me. This took place in Libya where mass protests were being held that called for the overthrow of the dictator, Colonel Gaddafi. It was reported that Gaddafi, on hearing of the protests and perhaps recalling his own revolutionary past, is said to have wanted to join the protestors and to stand with them. Clearly in the case of Gaddafi and the *Arab Spring*, he was mistaken. However, in contrast to Gaddafi, God is a God who is indeed on the side of the protestors. He demonstrates this in the book of Job and perhaps also through the cross.

Berish is a Job-like figure in this story. He is trying to make sense of his suffering. Like Job, his desire is to put God on trial and the play is a dramatic account of how this trial might play out. In this trial, Berish blames God for the suffering that he has witnessed. Berish is similar to Job in this sense but goes further than Job ever did. In contrast to the happy ending of the book of Job, Berish's story ends as the killers who have carried out the pogrom break into the inn "accompanied by deafening and murderous roars" – the pogrom continues.

**Jesus weeps over Lazarus and takes Martha's blame**

Since I first considered it, I have always found the story of Lazarus to be both deeply moving and fascinating. Here was a man who had died and had remained dead for three days. Jesus then raised him from the dead and thus the story ends. What the Bible does not tell us is what happened to Lazarus next. Presumably he must have lived for a while and then died again. And here lies my fascination – what becomes of a man who has suffered death once and knows that he must suffer it again. The experience of death may have been traumatic for Lazarus, and unusually, he would have to go through it a second time. Did he look forward to it in the sure knowledge of the resurrection of which he'd had a foretaste? Or did he dread it and the pain of it?

There is a theme in the story of Lazarus that reveals something of God's attitude to suffering. The story takes place in John 11 in which Jesus hears a report that his friend, 'the one you love', is ill. Now instead of going straight away to Lazarus to heal him, in verse 6 we find that Jesus delays for "two more days". Jesus' two-day delay means that when he finally arrives in Bethany, Lazarus is already dead. What's more, this appears to have been what Jesus intended through the delay.

In verse 21 Martha, Lazarus' grieving sister, says to Jesus that Lazarus would not have died if Jesus had been there. There is surely a hint of blame in Martha's words, which might be paraphrased as, 'Why weren't you here? If you had been here this wouldn't have happened – Lazarus wouldn't have died! It's your fault.' Then in verse 22, Martha shows great faith in saying that she still knows that God will do what Jesus asks. The story implies that Martha's accusation in verse 21 was not wrong. Lazarus would have lived if Jesus had been there. Jesus doesn't respond to her accusation and so tellingly he does not rebuke her.

Let us pause the story here. Jesus, through his inaction, has allowed a friend of his, whom he loves, to suffer death. Jesus then grieves over this death and suffering. This is a challenging point to take from the story – God is to blame, at least for some suffering, through his inaction. That is where theodicy begins – God allows some suffering to take place. In verse 35 we have the shortest verse in the Bible which shows God's response: "Jesus wept." It doesn't end there for God. Whilst God allows suffering, He also grieves for and suffers with those who suffer because He loves them. God is not dispassionate and removed – He enters in to the human drama. So remember, in your suffering, that the shortest, most memorable verse in the Bible shows God's response to suffering – He weeps.

When we weep for another, if it is genuinely for another and not in fact weeping for ourselves, then we not only sympathise with the other but we empathise with them. We feel their pain alongside them. Those are the kind of tears that I believe Jesus shed in John 11. They are a foreshadowing of the blood that he would shed on the cross when, by having chosen to live and die as a man and to ultimately give his life on the cross, he chose to suffer alongside all those he loves. It was on the cross that God allowed Himself to be defined as a God who suffers. By suffering in this way, all can now look to Him and see that God suffers also and hence that God suffers alongside them. In John 11, Jesus takes on the consequences of one man's suffering – through his grief – but on the cross he takes on the consequences of all suffering and sin.

I have of course, paused the story of Lazarus at the mid-point but now let's follow the story through to the end and so bring out a further important thought. Jesus goes on to raise Lazarus from the dead. It is a resurrection that prefigures his own resurrection as well as the general resurrection when we will all be raised. So, in the midst of suffering let us not forget that the story does not end with death but with life. Writing about the problem of evil without the redemption that comes through this resurrection is incomplete.

## Can we shout at God?

It is with great trepidation that I begin to write this section. Over the course of this book I have looked at various people who have complained to God. First and foremost in the book of Job, where Job lambasts God for his suffering, is initially rebuked by God, but then later is commended by God as the only one who spoke what was right (Job 42: 7). Secondly, there are Job's friends who argue vociferously in God's defence but then are rebuked by God for not saying what was right (again, Job 42:7). Then there is C.S. Lewis, the widower, mourning the loss of his wife and struggling with his Creator. Next is Ivan Karamazov, the doomed atheist, who wants to 'return his ticket' to God but who meets the Christ-like response of a kiss. The Grand Inquisitor stands with Ivan, accusing Christ and again is met with a kiss. Tesie appeared to struggle in her suffering between putting on a brave face and experiencing deep depression. Finally the Jewish people and others who suffered tremendously under the Nazis and continued in the line of Job by insisting on their right to complain, to put God on trial. All these people cried out to God and they were met by a God who heard them.

Being angry with God, shouting at God is, in a sense, being in relationship with God. But this is not a relationship of equals and we must be forever conscious of the majesty of God. Roger Forster cautions us against raging with God since although God can of course *handle it*, it is not Christ-like behaviour and, he argues, it is not what Job does.[88] Forster argues that Job is actually ranting and raving against the false god that his friends are proposing in their theodicies. I am not sure that I can agree with Forster's argument here for when Job yearns to take God to court, he is not referring to the false gods of his friends but to the true God that he knows and loves (Job 9: 33) – otherwise his yearning would be nonsensical. Nevertheless, Forster's point must be heeded; we must always be reverent to God and cautious of irreverence.

A contrasting view is shown by the words of Bishop Handley Moule who, reflecting on the cries contained in the book of Habakkuk ("How long, Lord, must I call for help, but you do not listen?" Habakkuk 1: 2) encouraged frank dialogue with God,

> to speak to Him all that is in the burdened soul, just as it is. The New Testament repeatedly speaks of the "boldness," the "access with confidence," to which we are invited as we draw near the Holy One. In the Greek, in many of these places, a notable word used by the Apostles: parrhesia [παρρησία], that is to say, literally, the freedom which can "say anything," telling out the very thought, unrelieved, exactly as it is. It was parrhesia indeed when Habakkuk said,

"Why do I pray to Thee, and it seems to result in nothing?" His awful trial told hard on him. He felt as perhaps he should not have felt. But he was perfectly right in telling out his feelings, right *or wrong*, to his Lord. For he was free to "say anything" to Him. And we, we in the light of our revealed nearness to Him in Christ, we indeed are meant to "say anything" to Him, feeling the bewilderment, "but knowing Whom we have believed."[89]

Paul Bradbury presents a good example of the misgivings that can arise from becoming angry with God. Having lost his temper with God due to the suffering of his child, he described his feelings,

This burst of anger affected us profoundly. I had never found myself to be angry with God in the way that I was that day. I had never uttered such words before in that way, with real venom and real anguish, words that came not from the thinking part of me but straight from the feeling part of me. It was a surprising sensation but it also made me nervous, for suddenly I was exploring areas I had never been in before. It was also dangerous, because part of me thought that perhaps this was blasphemy and renunciation. I automatically felt almost ashamed at this outburst. I could sense the disapproval of a church whose evangelical culture finds little space for honest emotions, that illuminate the negative aspects of our experience as the people of God on this earth. Surely this wasn't progression but regression; I had finally rebelled like a teenager who can't take it anymore. Would I not therefore find myself punished for such an outburst? How could I speak with God like this and expect to get away with it?[90]

So where do we strike the balance then in how, or whether, we communicate our feelings of anger to God? Do we see them as sin and so seek to overcome them? Or do we express them to God with boldness as part of our open and honest relationship with him? Do we treat God as our Lord or do we treat God as our Father? Saying to God, 'I love and trust You but I'm also angry at what has happened and at why You didn't intervene' might be an appropriate response. Such words can allow us to be truly honest with God about how we feel. Being honest with God is surely a part of being in a relationship with God as our Father. But, on the other hand, losing one's temper with God, or with anyone, is not something that should be done lightly or frequently. If, having lost our tempers, we examine ourselves honestly in prayer and reflection, repenting where necessary, then we will hopefully achieve the right balance.

One further note on lost tempers, there are times in relationships when arguments can serve a purpose since they can act as a vent for things that need to be said, which would otherwise be festering within. Arguments can also

be destructive, they can lead to things being said that are
not true but instead are intended to inflict pain. Just as we
must be careful what we say in our human relationships
when we have lost our tempers we must all the more be
careful what we say in prayer to God for God is not our
equal. Where we have wronged God in our words or
thoughts, we must repent. It is for this reason that we must
always be cautious in losing our temper with God but
should also know that He hears us and is with us.

## Can we distance God from this mess?

Many writers go to great lengths to separate God from the
causes of suffering in order to shield God from
responsibility. They do this by placing as great a distance
as possible between God and evil in order to deny any
link. Such writers tend to employ the freewill defence –
using the independent freewill of created beings to explain
evil whilst side-stepping the fact that God created them as
such. Indeed, John Hick argues that there is a distinction
to be made in relation to the responsibility for evil
between the freewill (Augustinian) and the soul-making
(Irenaean) defences,

> The main motivating interest of the
> Augustinian tradition is to relieve the
> Creator of responsibility for the
> existence of evil by placing that
> responsibility upon dependent beings
> who have wilfully misused their God-
> given freedom. In contrast the
> Irenaean type of theodicy ...accepts
> God's ultimate omni-responsibility
> and seeks to show for what good and
> justifying reason He has created a
> universe in which evil was inevitable.[91]

Whilst I agree with Hick's point above, I think that there is an element of similarity between the defences here for both seek to justify evil by arguing that God has a good reason for it. In the Augustinian freewill defence, it is freewill that is the greater good but with the negative side-effect of evil. Under the Irenaean soul-making defence, the worth of evil is even more evident – evil is worthwhile for Irenaeus because it improves our souls.

If evil is worthwhile, is it any less evil? Have these theodicies essentially led us to the conclusion that the evil we perceive is not in fact evil but is, in a sense, good? The question that haunts these theodicies is whether they agree with the Biblical triple affirmation that evil is indeed evil.

The issue of responsibility is, as John Roth points out, important,

> Do not take lightly what God's responsibility entails. It means: in the beginning ...Auschwitz. The point is not that God predestined or caused such events directly ...[rather under the freewill defence,] that freedom – despite what some thinkers would like – does not remove God from the dock.[92]

Roger Forster on the other hand, in his book, *Suffering and the love of God*, discusses the book of Job and its theology. For Forster a key part of the book is the description by God of Behemoth and Leviathan in chapters 40 and 41. Forster argues that Behemoth and Leviathan are satanic forces that man has been unable to control, "Man should have taken authority over him [Satan] as one of these beasts over whom God had given dominion. But instead, by obeying him, man gave the devil more authority on the earth."[93] Hence, the cause of evil and suffering in the world is the battle between humankind and the satanic cosmic forces. Both humans and satanic forces are free agents in this battle, which therefore creates a distance between God and the evil that exists.

Greg Boyd wrote a book on the problem of evil that directly addresses whether God is responsible – *Is God to blame?* Using the freewill defence, Boyd argued that God cannot prevent all evil because of the freewill that he has given to humankind. God has therefore limited himself by giving people freewill. So, Boyd asks, couldn't it be argued that God is responsible for evil because He has chosen to limit himself and create free beings?[94] Boyd made three points in response to this.

Firstly, he argued, that God is no more morally responsible for evil than parents are for the evil actions of their adult children. I am not entirely convinced by this argument since parents, if they have brought up their children badly, would, on some levels, be morally responsible if those children went on to commit evil acts. This would be an extreme example, but the point is that the environment and family that parents choose to bring their children up in does have ramifications on the behaviour of the children in later life. In a similar way, God has created the environment and circumstances into which we are born and it is these that will influence how we behave. Furthermore, unlike the parents, it is God who has determined that we should have freewill and so be able to commit evil and so His role in the process is significant.

Secondly, Boyd made the point that, God could be held responsible only if the "risk of creating this kind of world outweighed the gains".[95] Boyd seems to be saying here that God is only at fault for allowing evil if the gift of freewill turns out to be bad overall because of its evil consequences. However, this does not deny that God is still responsible for both the good and the evil that results from His creation rather this argues that it was, overall, good.

Thirdly, Boyd made the point that, "God nevertheless takes responsibility for evil. This is what the cross and resurrection of Jesus Christ are all about. God is not morally responsible for evil, but He voluntarily suffers the full force of evil in order to free creation from evil".[96] This response is not really a defence of God as responsible but is nevertheless an important point that I will be discussing further in the chapter *The cross – God takes the consequences*. Nevertheless, I do not think that Boyd's three arguments remove God from the dock.

A third thinker on God's responsibility is Hick. Hick begins by contrasting a God who permits evil to happen with a God who wills evil to happen. Hick argues that God permits evil to happen on a broad scale by His creation of free beings and on an individual level by not intervening via miracles when some evil is about to be committed. This permitting God is very different to a God that wills evil to happen or perpetrates evil Himself. Such a God would surely not be consistent with the God of love that we know? Nevertheless, Hick concludes that, "the distinction between permitting and willing can have no validity when applied to the planning and creating of the physical universe by an omnipotent Being".[97] Hick here is saying that, since God determined the rules of the universe such as the creation of free beings, He is responsible for the consequences of these rules as if He intended these consequences himself. Hence the distinction between permitting and willing is, in fact, arbitrary. Later on Hick remarks that it is,

> an inescapable conclusion that the *ultimate* responsibility for the existence of sinful creatures and of the evils which they both cause and suffer, rests upon God Himself. For monotheistic faith there is no one else to share that final responsibility. The entire situation within which sin and suffering occur exists because God willed and continues to will its existence; and we must believe that from the first He has known the course that His creation would take.[98]

And so for Hick, Forster's argument that satanic forces directly cause evil, does not absolve God from the ultimate and indirect responsibility for it. Later on,[99] Hick uses the analogy of a person deliberately leaving alcohol out for a recovering alcoholic. Even though the alcoholic is responsible if he succumbs to this temptation, the person who leaves the alcohol in his path is also responsible. Hick is therefore insistent that placing responsibility for evil on God does not shift the blame for our own actions from ourselves. The alcoholic analogy serves to affirm this for both the alcoholic and the person that left the alcohol are responsible for the outcome. The analogy is, however, slightly flawed because the alcohol serves no good purpose. Freewill, on the other hand, has both good and bad consequences.

My own view is perhaps most influenced by Hick and Roth. I agree with Hick that it is inescapable to conclude that God is ultimately responsible for evil and so, 'In the beginning ...Auschwitz'.

God in Pain

John Henry Moule Chamberlain

# The shouting of the voices

Before I detail what I think is the best response to the problem of evil in the next chapter, it would be worthwhile recalling many of the people and views that we have met on the way. In my first chapter, *Why is evil a problem and what is theodicy?*, I raised the importance of discussion in detailing the problem of evil, and so this chapter presents a summary of the arguments of this book in the form of a discussion.

But before the discussion begins, any conversation about suffering must surely begin with silence – the silence of Shivah – the seven days and seven nights of Job and his friends whilst they sat and grieved his loss. It is a time to take stock of the situation and to dwell amidst it. For words, no matter how emotive, always carry a certain level of logic and reason, whilst silence is capable of being simply raw emotion.

Breaking the silence, Job raises his voice in protest against his maker for his loss. Job insists on his innocence and so maintains the injustice of his suffering. He rants and rages against God and demands to face Him in a court of law. And yet he refuses to curse God and die. Next Job's friends respond, firstly by arguing that Job's suffering is a result of the loving discipline of God who is trying to improve Job's soul through His correction. Next, and more extreme, they argue that Job's suffering is a punishment for his own sins. But still Job stands firm upon his innocence.

Finally, God responds to Job out of the storm and having initially admonished him, God then upholds Job and his words, thus demonstrating that God is on the side of the sufferer. The Bible itself is similarly elusive in its response since it affirms that evil is evil, that God is good and that God is all-powerful. It is this affirmation that causes the tension in which the problem of evil exists. As each of the three truths pull against the other two, we are tempted to ignore one truth in order to resolve the situation. The Bible however, by its triple affirmation, does not allow us to do this. The philosopher, Alvin Plantinga, argues that it is logically possible for all three statements to be true if God has a good reason for creating a world with evil. But what could this reason be? And does logic really matter when the problem itself is so emotive?

Then the theodicies respond, the Augustinians argue that the reason for the evil of the world is as a consequence of human freewill. Without this freewill we would be automatons – clockwork oranges. The Grand Inquisitor argues however that God was mistaken here – goodness should have been forced on people rather than leaving them free to choose. Humans in the form of the church and the Inquisition have had to take the role of force in the absence of God doing so. They have filled the void caused by this dereliction of duty. Jesus and Alyosha respond with a kiss.

Next the Irenaeans argue that the evil of the world is there for the refinement of our souls. We suffer and therefore we improve. But what about those that never improve – those that are not redeemed? Such questions appear to lead John Hick to conclude that everyone is saved. But there are further questions – why does so much suffering seem to be purposeless and not result in any soul-making? Why does so little good result from so much evil?

Sitting aloof at the side, Hume's character, Philo, argues that God is beyond the scope of human reason and so challenges the very idea of devising a theodicy and discussing the issue. God's purposes are unknown and so how can we know what Plantinga's *good reason* could be? Leibniz, on the other hand, argues that this world is the best of all possible worlds. But where Leibniz sees darkness as shadows that enhance a painting by creating contrast, Voltaire sees dark stains that ruin a masterpiece.

More sufferers raise their shouts – Berish, the victim of a Jewish pogrom, in semi-fulfilment of Job's yearning, stages a mock trial of God and finds Him guilty. Some Jews in Auschwitz likewise find God guilty under the terms of His covenant with them. The mother of the servant child who was torn to shreds by the Russian General's hounds weeps. The murdered babies are silent. Tesie dies with great courage but cannot always overcome her depression as she suffers. Martha says to Jesus, "Lord, ...if you had been here, my brother would not have died"

(John 11: 21). These sufferers have advocates, Ivan Karamazov demands to hand back his ticket to God – he wants no part of anything that is built upon the suffering of an innocent. Their shouts are deafening. Moishe the Beadle, who saw power in the asking of questions, sits near and listens to the discussion.

And then C.S. Lewis identifies the ditch. He knows the philosophy and the theology but when tragedy strikes his own life, it is not nearly adequate. He can only cry out in pain and deep depression at his suffering. The lessons that he taught in his books do not seem to help for they are on one side of the ditch and he now finds himself on the other side.

And in the midst of all this suffering, all these voices and all these accusations, stands the cross. After having cried out, "My God, my God, why have you forsaken me?" (Matthew 27: 46), there is silence on the cross. It is the silence of a dead man hanging on a tree. It is the Bible's ultimate and final expression of the problem of evil. It demonstrates that evil is evil, that God is good and that God is all-powerful.

# The Cross – God takes the consequences

The Bible is unique in its response to the problem of evil because of the cross. The cross addresses evil in a way unlike any other theological response. In the cross, God not only defeats evil, but participates in the suffering that evil has caused. Sir John Polkinghorne, the physicist and theologian, reflected on this in a speech he gave in 2003,

> A Christian understanding of God's relationship to suffering is not that God is simply a compassionate spectator looking down on the strange and bitter world that God holds in being. As a Christian, I believe that God is participating in the suffering in the world, that God is truly a fellow sufferer. The Christian God is the crucified God. That is a very deep and mysterious, though, I believe, true,

> insight. That is the deep level at which
> the problem of suffering has to be met,
> and the possibility for religious belief
> really, for me, rests at that level.[100]

The cross reveals the heart of Job's God and so locates God in Auschwitz, suffering alongside the victims.

### The cross as God's sentence

At the cross, humankind, in the form of the Roman soldiers and the Sanhedrin, has judged God and concluded that, "it is better for one man [God] to die than that the whole nation may perish" (John 11: 50). The cross is the punishment inflicted upon God that follows this judgement. It is as if the trial of God that Ellie Wiesel imagined has actually happened and the sentence is passed on the cross. God is indeed found guilty and executed. By taking on our sins through the cross, God takes on the worst consequences of them and stands in our place, as well as suffering alongside us.

My own theodicy is the story of the cross. But it is not like the other theodicies. How can the execution of God be described as a justification of God? Through this story, it is as if God is saying to us,

> I am going to create a universe in
> which evil is done. It is going to result
> in each one of you sinning and falling
> short. These sins will lead to
> tremendous harm being done to
> yourselves and to each other. Some of
> you will kill, maim, rape, butcher and
> slay others. Some will even do this in
> my name. All of you will die, some

horribly. There will be great suffering
and so you will question me and even
question my existence. But to prove to
you that this universe is worth it, that
it has value and that each and every
one of you has value, I am going to
suffer alongside you. At the cross, I
will suffer the worst kind of death,
horrendous physical pain and,
alongside this, a spiritual crisis
through a separation within the
Godhead. It was not without reason
that Jesus cried out "My God, my
God, why have you forsaken me?"
(Mark 15: 34). I cannot take away
your suffering, to do so would take
away your life, but equally I am
absolutely not prepared to sit on my
throne and watch my children suffer
alone. I will be with you in this.

The cross is both an emotional and philosophical response
to the problem of evil and so it can dwell in that great and
ugly ditch between the two sides. It is emotional since it
speaks to our very being and continues to influence,
comfort and inspire us. How many worship songs have
been sung reflecting on the *wondrous cross*? The cross
shows God's heart, which is broken and its brokenness is
for us. So the anger that we feel at the violence and
suffering in the world is answered by the violence and
suffering that was expressed on the cross and was inflicted
on the body of Jesus Christ.

The cross is also a philosophical, theological and
intellectual response to the problem of evil since it

explains how evil and suffering are redeemed and defeated. Its interpretation is the subject of academic inquiry. Thus the cross allows for a common language of communication to be spoken and understood between the academic side of the ditch and the emotional side.

## Responding to the cries

Turning back to the shouting of the voices contained in the previous chapter, the cross enters into this conversation about evil as an active participant. It responds to the voices through its demonstration of divine love. The cross reveals a God who sits in the midst of Job, Berish, Auschwitz, the grieving Russian mother, Tesie, Martha and C.S. Lewis in silent suffering alongside – in Shivah. By taking the consequences of sin on Himself, God refuses to accept others' defences of Him and so rebukes Job's friends. The cross demonstrates that the evil and suffering in the world is in some way worth it – that there is a purpose and meaning behind it whether that be freewill, soul-making or another. The cross accepts the Grand Inquisitor's sentence whilst demonstrating that forcing people to obey is not the way. The cross answers Philo by showing the face of God and thus making God accessible to humankind. The cross shows Leibniz that the world is not the best of all possible worlds but that it is a world that is capable of redemption. Finally, the cross allows Moishe the Beadle, Berish and Ivan Karamazov to protest; it justifies their protest and it responds to their cries in sympathy as an act of love.

## A question of trust

God has created a universe that includes evil and suffering. Whether the suffering is the result of freewill, or is because of the soul-making process, is in some ways irrelevant here for the issue is that there is suffering and whether God has a good reason for it. In the chapter *But why me?* I referred to Stephen Davis' reflection that, "ultimately, it comes down to trust"[101] and I affirm Stephen Davis' point here. For our answer to the question of whether God has a good reason for creating the universe as it is will largely be determined by whether we trust God. It is the cross that allows us to trust God since He has proved His trustworthiness by taking part in His creation and taking on the consequences of His decision to create the universe as such. If God thinks that creation is worth going to the cross and suffering for then surely the value of our own lives are also worth our suffering for? Tim Keller reflects on the issue of trust and the cross,

> Only Christianity, of all the world's major religions, teaches that God came to earth in Jesus Christ and became subject to suffering and death Himself. See what this means? Yes, we do not know the reason God allows evil and suffering to continue, or why it is so random, but now at least we know what the reason is not. It cannot be that He does not love us. It cannot be that He does not care. He is so committed to our ultimate happiness that He was willing to plunge into the greatest depths of suffering Himself. He understands us, He has been there, and He assures us that He has a plan to eventually wipe away every tear. Someone might say, "But that's only half an answer to the question 'Why?'" Yes, but it is the half we need.[102]

Keller also quotes Ann Voskamp who makes the same point in a more poetic way,

> If trust must be earned, hasn't God unequivocally earned our trust with the bark on the raw wounds, the thorns pressed into the brow, your name on the cracked lips? How will He not also graciously give us all things He deems best and right? He's already given us the incomprehensible.[103]

Fundamentally, the God that suffers and dies on the cross is the God that can be trusted.

## The redeeming nature of the cross

The cross was not the end for Jesus and it is not the end for us. For in the cross, God was not only present amidst the ultimate expression of evil on earth, He was also redeeming it through, first His death, and then His resurrection. This serves as a metaphor for the world, whilst there is indeed bleak and terrible suffering and evil at work within it, there is also redemption. As Hick says, "throughout the Biblical history of evil, including even this darkest point, God's purpose of good was moving visibly or invisibly towards its far-distant fulfilment".[104]

On the cross, God turns evil to good via the painful process of death and resurrection. Indeed, the gospels say that God intended the cross from the start of Jesus' ministry (Luke 9:22) and even before Jesus was born (Isaiah 53). This was always the redeeming plan at the heart of God. It was a plan with harsh consequences in the form of crucifixion; but these were consequences that would be borne, not by humankind, but by God himself.

Therefore, when considering the cross and when considering suffering in general, we must also consider redemption.

## Christus Victor

One interpretation of how the cross atones for our sins, which is most complementary to my theodicy, is that of Christus Victor. Christus Victor is perhaps the earliest interpretation of the crucifixion and was the predominant interpretation for the first thousand years of Christianity however the term itself was coined by Gustaf Aulén as the title of his book published in 1931. Aulén is credited with reinvigorating this earlier belief.

Christus Victor draws on the theme of ransom that is mentioned in the New Testament. The gospel of Mark (10: 45) states, "For even the Son of Man did not come to be served, but to serve, and to give his life as a ransom for many" and 1 Timothy (2: 5–6) says, "Christ Jesus, who gave himself as a ransom for all people." It is the Christus Victor model that arose from Christians trying to make sense of such language. What does the Bible mean by its references to ransom? Origen, an early church father, argued that the ransom must have been paid to someone, but to whom? He argued that it must be to Satan, since God was not holding sinners to ransom. Gregory the Great, another early church father, developed this idea further by arguing that God had tricked Satan into accepting Christ's life as payment for the ransom on humanity. Because Christ was divine and sinless, his life not only paid the ransom but also defeated Satan, since Satan had accepted too great a ransom. Other writers then developed the idea further such that it was viewed that Christ had obtained a victory over Satan and death through his own death and resurrection.

This victory was often seen as being the outcome of a battle between Jesus and Satan. The idea of battle draws on such verses as 1 Corinthians 15: 24–26, which says, "Then the end will come, when he [Jesus] hands over the kingdom to God the Father after he has destroyed all dominion, authority and power. For he must reign until he has put all his enemies under his feet. The last enemy to be destroyed is death." It is also shown in the book of Revelation, which tells of the triumph of the lamb. Furthermore, the foretold One who will crush the serpent's head (Genesis 3: 15) employs the same imagery of victory over Satan.

The horrors of World War I and its demonstration of the reality of evil rekindled the popularity of the Christus Victor model presumably because it was comforting to think of Christ fighting against the devil and evil when people were in the midst of their own battles. Blocher draws from the Christus Victor model when he says,

> Evil is conquered as evil because God turns it back upon itself. He makes the supreme crime, the murder of the only righteous person, the very operation that abolishes sin. The manoeuvre is utterly unprecedented. No more complete victory could be imagined. God responds in the indirect way that is perfectly suited to the ambiguity of evil. He entraps the deceiver in his own wiles. Evil, like a judoist, takes advantage of the power of good, which it perverts; the Lord, like a supreme champion, replies by using the very grip of the opponent. So is

> fulfilled the surprising verse: 'With
> the pure you show yourself pure; and
> with the crooked you show yourself
> perverse' (Ps. 18:26).[105]

It is this imagery of battling with evil within the Christus Victor model that best complements my theodicy. For on the cross, Jesus aggressively battles against evil on our behalf and alongside us. He stands and fights with us. That evil needs to be defeated in a physical as well as a spiritual way confirms its seriousness – the evilness of evil. That Jesus battles on the cross for our sakes shows the goodness of God. That Jesus ultimately triumphs over evil demonstrates that God is all-powerful.

### Job's friends imitate the cross
Turning back to Job's friends, as we discussed earlier, their response to Job was twofold. Firstly, they spent time with him when they sat in silence, tore their clothes and sprinkled dust on their heads as a sign of their mourning with him (Job 2: 11–13). This lasted a week, during which no words were spoken. Their second response was in conversation with Job as they sought to give answers on behalf of God in response to Job's accusations. Their first response was compassionate as they suffered alongside Job. Their second response was condemnatory as they placed the blame for Job's suffering on his own head.

However, those initial seven days of silence, of weeping and mourning, correspond closely to my interpretation of the cross here. For on the cross, Jesus participates in human suffering and so suffers alongside us. The cross speaks into our suffering, not with words, but as a beautiful, yet terrible, picture of the love of God for us.

Hence, those who sympathise and sit alongside sufferers, are a picture of the work of Jesus on the cross.

## God suffers with us

The cross of Christ has been a source of solace for the weak and downtrodden throughout history. Perhaps the most famous group to record their suffering were the African slaves kidnapped and taken across the ocean to the United States of America and Caribbean. Given the cross, it is not surprising that they were able to sing, 'Nobody knows the trouble I've seen, nobody knows but Jesus'.

The cross has always told such people, 'I am with you. I suffer with you'. It is because of the cross therefore that people in desperate situations, who are forgotten by the rest of the world, know that they are remembered by the God who is with them. He is the God who came down from heaven to be with us. The God who died the most horrific of deaths, abandoned by His friends and despised by those around Him.

No matter what our death, no matter what suffering we experience, we know that our Lord went before us. He experienced it and He understands. We know that our suffering need not be a sign of failure of having done something wrong or of weakness for our Lord did none of those and yet He suffered. We know also, through Jesus' resurrection, that there is hope and restoration, if not in this life then in the next.

I am so thankful for the many aspects of the cross that I keep discovering the more I consider it. Just as a picture can paint a thousand words, so the story of the cross can be interpreted and reinterpreted and bring new and fresh insights into our lives. As we suffer, it brings comfort. As we sin, it brings justice. As we doubt, it brings hope. We have a unique faith, one where God suffers and dies for us. Let us never forsake this.

## Life is Beautiful

The film, *La Vita e Bella*, gives a picture of love in the midst of suffering. The film is set in Italy during the Second World War. In it, a Jewish man, Guido, marries an Italian lady, Dora, and they have a son. Eventually the Nazis come to take Guido away to the concentration camps. Discovering that her husband has been taken, Dora rushes to the train station only to find that he has been loaded onto a train along with their son and that it is bound for the camp. Having failed to get him released from the train, she then demands to be let on to the train herself. Since she is not Jewish and so has no reason to be on the train, the Nazis are reluctant to let her on but she insists and is eventually let on. This of course leads to her being taken to the concentration camp along with her husband and son.

There is a sense in which Dora's action here is futile. It leads to her suffering greatly and needlessly and ultimately contributes towards the death of Guido who is shot towards the end of the film when he tries to make sure that Dora is alive. However, there is another sense in which it is the most meaningful, courageous and good thing that Dora could do. She refused to let her husband and son suffer alone but demanded that she should suffer alongside them. I have always admired Dora's act of self-sacrifice. I would like to think that, presented with the same circumstances, I too would demand to get on the train. I am thankful that God likewise demands to suffer alongside. For God does not sit in heaven, impassively observing the suffering of His creatures. Rather God demands to suffer alongside them.

There is another point that the film makes, which is shown in its title. For life *is* beautiful. Shockingly, the film is a comedy, but this genre somehow works for the subject matter and indeed increases the poignancy of the message. However, as C.F.D. Moule said, even in the midst of evil, goodness can spring up.[106] It sneaks in, almost undetected, but it is there. Amidst the pain and suffering of Auschwitz, there was also goodness and undoubted acts of true heroism and self-sacrifice. The sacrifices both of Dora and of Guido displayed in the film make this point.

### The parallel narratives
When hearing of the heart-breaking tragedies that friends and family have experienced, I am always tempted to seek to provide an answer. I am wrong to do so and this book has failed if the reader views it as an answer to suffering. For, whether theologically correct or not, answers are liable to shut down the expression of suffering and therefore deny the validity of the hurt being expressed by the sufferer. Is an answer even needed when someone suffers? I strongly believe that the cross gives an alternative approach to suffering. It does not end the cries of the sufferer or invalidate them in any way. Although the cross is the ultimate response, it does not deny the truth of questions. God does not silence the story of one's suffering nor alter one iota of it. However, in the cross, he reveals a parallel truth. This new truth does not deny or simply change the narrative of a person's suffering but instead, by running alongside the narrative of suffering, God's narrative completely transforms and redeems it.

I remember listening to a sermon once where the speaker, J John, described a conversation he had with an adult who had been traumatised by a childhood experience. The adult described their time as a young girl at school when a certain teacher took a disliking to them. Such was the cruelty of the teacher that on one occasion they arranged for the girl's classmates to write on the blackboard everything they thought was wrong with this child. One by one, each classmate stood up and wrote on the board: 'You're ugly', 'You smell', 'I don't like you', and so on it went. Even those children that the girl took to be friends joined in the abuse. This incident had left the child, now an adult, traumatised. J John counselled her, "There was something else that happened, that you didn't witness," he said, "After all the other children had written on the board, a man got up, Jesus. He walked up to the board and wiped out everything that had been written on it and he wrote, in letters that filled the board, 'I LOVE YOU'." The love of God, as demonstrated on the cross, can have a similar effect on us.

This truth that J John referred to; the parallel story of the book of Job where the Father expressed His pride in Job; the truth of the cross; these things all let us glimpse into the parallel narrative to our lives. It is a narrative of a God who loves us to such an extent that He would suffer and die for us. He is a God who wants to get His hands dirty in the sin and suffering of the world. He is not a God who could stand by and watch; He cares too much. And so, knowing this God, does not diminish the suffering that I experience but it does put it into context and, by doing so, transform it.

## The cross as narrative

I have deliberately tried in this book to make use of narrative, rather than statements, in discussing the problem of evil. The cross is also framed in the Bible as a story rather than a doctrine. This is immensely helpful for stories are open-ended and capable of multiple complementary interpretations. Stories enable and further discussion rather than closing conversation down. I believe that one of the reasons that Jesus spoke in parables was for this same purpose. By the cross, the innocent sufferer can take comfort that Christ also suffered in innocence and the guilty person can take comfort in the forgiveness of their sins achieved on the cross. We can talk, in Christian circles, of *bringing things to the cross* for the cross has become a symbol leading to meditation on the love and forgiveness of God as well as a means by which we approach God. All these things are made possible because the cross is not narrow dogma but open narrative. Likewise, as a story, the cross can speak to the heart in relation to the problem of evil rather than doctrine, which speaks to the head.

## A child is murdered

The story depicted in *Night* by Elie Wiesel includes a scene in a concentration camp where a child is murdered. It is appropriate to end this chapter with this. The murder occurs during roll call in the camp where three gallows have been set up in front of the thousands of prisoners. Two of the gallows are for adult prisoners but the third is for a child who has been arrested in connection with an act of sabotage. It is unclear whether or not he is guilty of this crime for he remained silent under the torture that preceded his death. Despite the shouts of his fellow condemned, the child remains silent at his execution. The prisoners who watch this tragedy are shocked and outraged by what they witness, "Where is merciful God, where is He?" one asks. The prisoners are then executed by hanging and whilst the two adults die swiftly, the child is not so fortunate. His rope still twitches more than half an hour after the hanging because the child doesn't weigh enough for his neck to break and thus enable a quick death. The prisoners walk past the child as he lingers in a state between life and death. As they walk, the author narrates:

> Behind me, I heard the same man asking:
> "For God's sake, where is God?"
> And from within me, I heard a voice answer:
> "Where He is? This is where –
> hanging here from this gallows…"[107]

This shocking story and the identification of the child with God are left open to several interpretations. The most obvious is that here, in this situation, God has died. This scene portrays the end, full stop. For how can God exist when such atrocities are being committed? Here God has abandoned His people because He has allowed this to happen. This scene, and indeed the holocaust itself, portrays the problem of evil in all its dreadfulness and challenges us as to whether we can hold a belief in a God that created a world in which such things happen.

There is however another interpretation that is possible. The child's execution in many respects mirrors that of Jesus, for the child is silent before his accusers and is executed along with two others who shout in protest. The child may therefore be identified with Jesus, as God. This identification reverses the emphasis of the story. God is there, on the gallows, suffering alongside. He loves people to such an extent that He comes down to be with them, and in the worst of circumstances, to identify with them. Jesus is with humanity now in its suffering and Jesus was with the child when he died.

The scene portrayed in *Night* leaves us with a stark choice: we can see evil as *proving* that God is dead or we can see God's death on the cross as *proving* that God is with us in the midst of evil. By allowing for both views, this story shows that perhaps these two alternatives are more closely aligned than we would at first think.

# Epilogue: the challenge of evil

**Are we hypocrites for even asking?**

Whilst writing this book I have become struck by the excuse that is inherent in the question of the problem of evil. We may ask, 'Why does God allow suffering?', but there is another, more immediate and far more relevant question, 'What are we doing about the suffering in the world?' Please do not misunderstand – I am not seeking here to undermine the question of the problem of evil – it is a valid question that is often asked from a place of pain. However, any who ask this question are guilty of hypocrisy if they do not also try to do all in their power to alleviate the suffering of others. Much suffering can be prevented through our own actions and if we seek to justify inaction by blaming God then we are surely at fault.

Christians especially should be acting on the suffering that they witness. Christians are the ambassadors of the kingdom of God and must therefore act out the will of God. When confronted with suffering, they must respond firstly by suffering alongside those who suffer – just as Jesus demonstrated. Secondly, again following the example of Jesus who stood against evil through his healing ministry and his exorcisms, they must stand against evil in their actions. In our own lives this stance may be through prayer, through social action, through feeding and housing the poor or through whatever means necessary but we must always stand against evil wherever we find it.

To the Christian, evil is not just an intellectual problem but a practical challenge. The philosopher may pontificate over the problem of evil but the Christian must embrace its challenge to show the love of God in a broken and fallen world. Let us not be armchair Christians like the armchair anthropologists of Victorian times who wrote theses about tribes on the other side of the world who they had never met but instead let us respond to our calling to engage with the world and to see suffering and evil as a challenge – we should mourn with those who mourn. We should not be like the ridiculed Leibniz, whose cosy existence prevented him from understanding the pain of the world, but we should instead be like Dora, who demanded to get on the train to the concentration camp.

**To mourn with those who mourn**
Throughout this book I have spoken of being with those who suffer. This is what Job's friends initially did by sitting in Shivah with him; this is what Alyosha did through his kiss to Ivan and Jesus through his kiss of the Grand Inquisitor. I commend you to do likewise because this is how we follow in the footsteps of Jesus.

N.T. Wright lays down the challenges that the cross and the gospel present to us, "The call of the gospel is for the church to *implement* the victory of God in the world *through suffering love*. The cross is not just an example to be followed; it is an achievement to be worked out, put into practice".[108] It is vitally important that Christians do indeed follow Jesus by displaying suffering love – putting others first; turning the other cheek; loving enemies; and mourning with those who mourn.

Mourning with those who mourn does not and should not, of course, always involve words or answers or fixes. Sometimes it is simply a question of dwelling in the ditch, where our brothers and sisters may find themselves. It is not always a comfortable thing, but then crosses rarely are.

God in Pain

# Appendix I: Part X and XI of Hume's Dialogues – a summary

Three characters take part in Hume's dialog on the problem of evil – Demea, Philo and Cleanthes. Demea has a religious stance and argues that we cannot come to know God through reason since God is beyond human comprehension. Philo comes to the same conclusion as Demea, but from a more philosophical, logical perspective. Finally, Cleanthes disagrees and instead argues that God is knowable by reason and so can be comprehended. All three are therefore believers in God, and so their quarrel is not over the existence of God, rather their quarrel is over how God is known or indeed whether He can be known. In relation to logic, Demea stands in contrast to the other two due to his more mystical, religious stance whilst Philo and Cleanthes are the arch-rationalists.

The discussion of the problem of evil begins with Demea and Philo agreeing that suffering is universal to all people.[109]

Demea paints a particularly depressing picture of life when he argues that "The first entrance into life gives anguish to the new-born infant and to its wretched parent …And it is at last finished in agony and horror".[110] In nature too there is violence with the strong preying upon the weak. Philo expands on Demea's point by arguing that although humankind is not preyed upon by other animals, this does not remove humanity's suffering since people instead create imaginary enemies for themselves through their fears and superstitions, such as their fear of death as well as through wars and violence. Additionally, people suffer internally from such things as despair, fear and dejection. Philo reflects that, although people suffer in their lives, they still cling to them for they are afraid of death. "This is the secret chain, say I, that holds us. We are terrified, not bribed to the continuance of our existence".[111] By stressing the suffering, which both Demea and Philo see all around them, they are of course setting the scene for a discussion of the problem of evil and how a good God could be compatible with it. They have now established the first of the triple affirmation – that evil exists.

Now it is the turn of the more cheerful Cleanthes who enters the discussion. Cleanthes claims that he does not feel such misery in his own life and so Demea and Philo are overstating their case. The others deride Cleanthes for this and challenge his anthropomorphic view of God. For Cleanthes had claimed in an earlier discussion that God's attributes, such as justice, wisdom and goodness, are of the same nature as the same virtues in humans so that an analogy can be drawn between God and man. Cleanthes' anthropomorphic claim here is crucial to Philo's argument against him.

Philo then states the problem of evil in its classic form – if God is wise, good and powerful then why are people unhappy? The existence of unhappy people and of suffering leads Philo to argue that God's benevolence cannot resemble the benevolence of people in the analogical sense that Cleanthes has claimed. If it did then He would have done something about the situation and so reduced or eliminated the suffering that we witness. Philo therefore uses the problem of evil, not to attack belief in God, but to drive a wedge into Cleanthes' belief that God's goodness is akin to humanity's goodness and, by extension, that God can be known by reason. By arguing that God's goodness must be of a different, incomprehensible type to humankind's goodness, Philo is arguing that both God and the reason for suffering are incomprehensible and therefore only knowable by faith. In other words, Philo's response to the problem of evil is to claim that God's goodness is not comprehensible to us whereas Cleanthes does not have the option of using such a defence since he believes in the knowability of God. This represents an attack on the goodness of God.

Cleanthes responds to this trap by arguing that if Philo can prove his point that humankind is unhappy and suffers in the world then he has not only disproved knowledge of God by reason but has also disproved religion and therefore God himself. Demea, who may be somewhat out of his depth in this discussion, objects to this by arguing that many explanations can be given for the suffering that occurs in this life, especially when it is seen in the light of eternity. Cleanthes objects to such a defence – we shouldn't argue that the explanation for suffering is something that is unseen and unprovable – an argument should only be made based on empirical evidence. Plantinga's no-seeums spring to mind here. An argument not based on empirical evidence can only ever be demonstrated to be possible and never actually be established as true. Therefore, to support his belief in the goodness of God, Cleanthes is forced to deny the suffering of the world for he cannot rely on unprovable explanations such as heaven. Cleanthes tries to alter the premises of the debate slightly by not denying the existence of pain but instead arguing that pleasure outweighs pain in the world and so he seeks to undermine the evilness of evil.

Responding to Cleanthes' attempt to change the debate, Philo counters that Cleanthes cannot even prove that pleasure outweighs pain in the world. Turning Cleanthes argument against him, Philo then says that since Cleanthes claims that religion relies upon this being true, Cleanthes has therefore only demonstrated that religion is unprovable and therefore uncertain. Philo next tracks back to attack Cleanthes' attempt to shift the debate by arguing that Cleanthes' belief in the understandability of God's motives suggests that an infinitely good God should behave as such. Hence, such a God would surely not simply create a world where pleasure outweighed pain but would rather create one without any pain whatsoever. Philo therefore sees Cleanthes' belief that God's motives are open to scrutiny and are understandable as untenable and so maintains his view that God must instead be mysterious.

Having listened to the onslaught of Philo, Part XI opens with Cleanthes' counter-attack on the view, shared by Demea and Philo, that God must be mysterious. He does so by arguing that Demea and Philo, through this belief, are denying the possibility of using analogy to talk about God. Without using analogy we cannot really talk about God at all since all our human words are insufficient for the task. How can the finite human word *goodness* describe the infinite goodness of God except by analogy to the goodness that we see on earth? Without analogy we would have no idea of what God is really like since we would have nothing to compare him to – no point of reference. All religious language must therefore make use of analogy to some extent. Hence, if we abandon analogy, Cleanthes contends, we must also abandon religious language and therefore religion.

Changing tack, Cleanthes suggests that a limited, finitely good God would be compatible with the existence of evil in the universe and asks Philo for his view. Philo uses a thought experiment to respond to Cleanthes: imagine that a rational being that was not in our universe was tasked with imagining what a universe would look like that had been created by a finitely good and all-powerful God. This rational being's expectation of what such a universe would look like would surely be very different to what the universe is actually like. Or, to approach from the opposite angle, if the rational being started in our own universe with the suffering that exists in it – would such a being conclude that it was created by a finitely good God? Similarly, Philo suggests, if we see a building where not one room is perfect, we blame the architect and we do not assume that he is perfect.

Philo then introduces four circumstances in which evil and suffering arise. None of them have obvious, good explanations or purposes but then the universe is complicated such that they may all have necessary reasons for their existence. If suffering has a purpose then presumably it is compatible with the existence of a good God, if it does not then how do we explain it? The first circumstance that Philo mentions is that our bodies often compel us to do things by inflicting pain on us via our senses. For example, the painful sensation of burning results in us preserving our lives by immediately moving away from fire. The self-preservation impulse is good, however the experience of pain is not. Philo therefore questions why our senses could not instead simply reduce the level of pleasure that we experience in order to compel us to good rather than doing so by inflicting pain on us. However, surely a being that only ever experienced pleasure of varying degrees might perceive their lower levels of pleasure to be the equivalent to what we experience as pain since they would not know actual pain to compare it to. Thus the effect would be the same.

The second of Philo's circumstances in which suffering arises is because the universe follows regular, uniform laws. The result of these laws is that if, for example, we trip up then the law of cause and effect means that we will fall and hurt ourselves. This law applies every time that we trip and so causes pain every time. Philo asks why God couldn't instead suspend these laws on every occasion when they would result in pain and so eliminate pain altogether from the universe. Alternatively, God could intervene in the universe to prevent some of the most significant sufferings, for example by preventing Hitler's birth (to give a more recent example), and so reduce the level of suffering in the universe.

The third circumstance that Philo mentions is related to creation. Philo argues firstly that all animals are created with just the right amount of physical and mental qualities in order to survive. In humankind's case this has resulted in people being much more intelligent than the animals but this is at the expense of people's physical prowess. People lack much of the strength and speed, as well as of course

John Henry Moule Chamberlain

the ability to fly, which many animals possess. This is the economy of creation – every species has just the right qualities, both physical and mental, to survive. Philo contrasts this with how an *indulgent parent* might create. Such a parent might bestow upon its creatures qualities that would guard against accidents and therefore ensure happiness in the creatures regardless of other circumstances. Even a small improvement in humankind could immeasurably improve the happiness of people. Though Philo does not mention it, this argument could also be linked to disease – an indulgent parent would surely have made people immune to cancer.

The fourth and final circumstance again relates to creation, but this time to its order. Philo begins by observing how well ordered and structured creation is – with its different parts interacting in complementary ways. However they do not interact perfectly, for example, the winds that assist sailing ships to travel the seas also result in lethal storms that wreck those same ships. Many of the qualities bestowed on creatures in the universe, such as love or ambition, when in excess or defective can result in misery. And so, the balance of the universe, when it is knocked slightly, may result in suffering.

Philo argues that these four circumstances result in the evil and suffering in the world and without them there would be no suffering in it. Philo cannot see why a good God could not alter these four circumstances and so eliminate suffering from the universe. Philo ponders at this stage how far to push his point. He cautiously concludes that the existence of these four circumstances in the universe is not incompatible with the existence of a good God since there could be some unknown explanation as to why all four are necessary and therefore *good* for the universe. Again,

Plantinga's no-seeums draw upon a similar notion. Philo therefore argues that we cannot know either way, since the existence of all four circumstances neither proves nor disproves the existence of a good God.

Next Philo discusses the possibility that both a good and a bad God could be inferred from the circumstances that the universe contains, and therefore explain the evil. Philo sees four options – a good God; a bad God; a good and a bad God; or a God with neither goodness nor badness. Since the phenomena of the universe are both good and bad, Philo discounts the first two. The third option is opposed by the "uniformity and steadiness of general laws [of the universe]"[112] and so Philo sees the fourth option, that God is neither good nor bad, as the most probable.

Philo is not here arguing against the existence of God – he is simply arguing against Cleanthes' view that an analogy can be drawn between humankind's goodness and God's goodness and so against the affirmation that God is good. The implication of Philo's view is that God's goodness is so different from humankind's that, in human terms, it is neither good nor bad. Philo sums up his argument by saying that anthropomorphites like Cleanthes must assign a cause for the evil in the world and that cause can only, ultimately, be God.

Demea objects to Philo's argument. He had originally sided with Philo due to their common belief in the mysteriousness of God but he now sees that Philo's views ultimately lead to heresy and perhaps atheism. Part XI concludes with Demea, making his excuses and leaving the discussion.

# Appendix II: A summary of the discussion contained in the book of Job

In writing this book I began by studying the book of Job. Doing this gave me a solid foundation from which to approach the problem of evil. I had initially experienced difficulty in understanding this great book for the central dialogue in it is long and sometimes hard to follow. I therefore wrote the below summary of the dialogue from chapters 3 to 42 and doing so greatly helped me in getting to know this book. Hopefully it may also be useful to the reader. The summary below focuses on the dialogue not the narrative sections of the book.

Job 3: Having suffered terrible loss and after seven days sitting in silence with his friends, Job begins by cursing the day of his birth and wishing for death

Job 4–5: Eliphaz speaks first on behalf of Job's friends and starts by challenging Job by making the point that humans reap what they sow and those who sow evil, reap evil. Then in 4: 17 he asks "can a mortal be more righteous than God?" In 5: 1 he mocks Job "Call if you will, but who will answer you?" and therefore starts to reveal the gap that Jesus fills in the New Testament by being the one who answers. Eliphaz then suggests that if Job appeals to God, God will answer and then in 5: 17 suggests that God may be disciplining Job and so, once the discipline is complete, He will then restore him. Eliphaz is here arguing that Job's suffering is in the context of this loving discipline – it is not that Job is evil and so it is not punishment but rather is a correction.

Job 6–7: Job responds by saying that his suffering is from God (6: 4) but that he refuses to touch it (6: 7) and so he rejects the correction and calls on God to end his misery. Job complains that his friends are not helpful in his time of need (6: 14) and are not standing with him and comforting him. Job insists that he is righteous and so, in response to Eliphaz, his suffering cannot be God's loving correction (6: 29). Therefore Job insists on his right to complain about his suffering (7: 11). In 7: 17–21, Job addresses God, beginning by asking, "What is man that you make so much of him." For Job would rather that God did not intervene in his life with such torments but would instead just leave him alone for he does not want God's suffering. Job insists on his innocence, this time to God (7: 20). It is interesting here that neither Job, nor his friends, ever question whether the suffering comes from God for they do not know the back story in the heavenly court and its satanic origin.

Job 8: Bildad speaks next and says that God is righteous. If Job is pure and upright (8: 6) and pleads with God then God will restore him to an even more plentiful position than before. This is of course essentially what happens to Job and so Bildad is inadvertently correct here.

Job 9–10: Job agrees with Bildad but asks "how can anyone be righteous before God?" (9: 2). How can Job plead his case with God, the creator of the universe? Job could only plead for mercy from God but he wouldn't even get a hearing (9: 15–16). Even though Job knows that he is blameless, he knows that God cannot be questioned. Job argues that God is unjust for "He destroys both the blameless and the wicked" (9: 22). God is responsible for the suffering of the world for "if it is not He, then who is it?" (9: 24). Job yearns to be able to confront God in court but recognises the impossibility of this for it is not a contest between equals, "if only there were someone to arbitrate between us ...Then I would speak up without fear of Him, but as it now stands with me, I cannot" (9: 33, 35). As with Eliphaz's earlier comment, Job is here highlighting the gap that Jesus will later fulfil (1 John 2: 1). Then in chapter 10, Job seems to plead with God as if in court asking for God to declare what charges He has against him (10: 2).

Job 11: Next Zophar speaks up and bemoans the fact that God lets Job's accusations go unanswered. Then he talks about the mysteries of God (11: 7) and claims that God is in fact righteous for Job is at fault (11: 10–12). If Job ceases to sin (11: 14) then he will be restored. Thus none of Job's friends believe his claim that he is not at fault. They all argue that he has in some way brought his suffering upon himself.

Job 12–14: The conversation starts to become understandably more heated as Job responds by insisting that he is righteous (12: 4) and that God has inflicted the suffering upon him (12: 9) for God is ultimately in control (12: 13–25). Job again wants to argue his case with God (13: 3) for it is God who he sees as his real challenger not his friends who are merely seeking to defend God. It would therefore be better that Job's friends were silent (13: 5) for they speak deceitfully on behalf of God (13: 7). Job desires two things from God: that God withdraws His hand from him (13: 21) and that he be allowed to contest with God over his suffering as if in a court (13: 22).

Job 15: Eliphaz begins his second attempt to persuade Job of his error by accusing Job of lying due to the corruption of his sins (15: 5) for no man is truly pure as Job claims (15: 14–16). It is the wicked that suffer torment for their sins (15: 20). Thus, as positions become entrenched, Eliphaz shifts his argument from the softer view that God is lovingly correcting Job to the harder view that God is punishing Job for his wickedness.

Job 16–17: Job answers and again states that God is responsible for his suffering (16: 12). Job then talks prophetically of an advocate in heaven who, unknown to Job, is Jesus, "Even now my witness is in heaven: my advocate is on high. My intercessor is my friend as my eyes pour out tears to God; on behalf of a man he pleads with God as a man pleads for his friend" (16: 19–21). It is poignant also that this advocate is doing precisely what Job's three friends should have been doing – pleading Job's case in prayer before God.

Job 18: However Bildad is unwavering and restates his view that those who suffer are evil.

Job 19: Job says that if his suffering is due to his sin then it is his business alone (19: 4) but insists that God has wronged him (19: 6). Job bemoans that God does not respond to his accusations (19: 7) and restates that his suffering is God's fault (19: 11). But there is some hope for again Job speaks prophetically of Jesus, "I know that my Redeemer lives, and that in the end he will stand upon the earth" (19: 25).

Job 20: Zophar is unmoved and says that the godless are punished and so their joy is brief.

Job 21: Job then widens his complaint to God by describing the general injustice of the world. The wicked prosper even though they reject God (21: 7) and God rarely punishes them (21: 17–21). Job then complains about the injustice that some suffer whilst others prosper for no apparent reason (21: 23–26). Job finally accuses his friends of speaking nonsense and lies (21: 34).

Job 22: Eliphaz insists then that Job is wicked (22: 5) and goes on to accuse Job of not looking after the poor and needy (22: 7). Eliphaz then argues that righteous people should rejoice in their own ruin – presumably because they should trust God and so know that they will be restored (22: 19). This contrasts with Job who does not rejoice in his suffering and so by implication cannot be righteous. Eliphaz then encourages Job to submit to God so that he may be restored (22: 21) and he implies that the restoration may not be in relation to physical goods but may instead be spiritual (22: 24–25) – Job will then learn to rejoice in his suffering. This is perhaps the most offensive argument that Job's friends have used so far.

Job 23–24: Job maintains his innocence and that he wants to face God in court (23: 3–4) but is frustrated that he cannot (24: 1). Job then describes the sin and injustice of the world (24: 2) that at many times goes unpunished (24: 12). Eventually though all evil men will die and rot (24: 19). Job's point is that although the evil may prosper in this life, in the end they will die.

Job 25: Bildad responds by saying that God is great so how can any man be righteous before God.

Job 26–31: Job commences a long monologue by describing God's terrifying greatness (26: 7–14). But then Job restates his claim that God has treated him unjustly (27: 2) and insists on the truth of his own words of defence (27: 4) as well as his righteousness (27: 6). Job next echoes the arguments of his friends by describing how God punishes the godless (27: 13–23). Job then uses the metaphor of men searching for precious metals in a mine to describe the search for wisdom – for that is what Job and his friends are seeking in their discussion (28: 12). Ultimately Job concludes that wisdom comes from God – "the fear of the Lord – that is wisdom" (28: 28). Job then longs for happier times, when he was respected by others and helped others (29: 2) but now Job is mocked by people. Even the sons of those who are outcasts mock him (30: 1–14). But now Job suffers and is close to death (30: 16). Job cries out to God but He does not answer (30: 20) and instead inflicts pain upon Job (30: 21). Job again yearns for a trial – for God to "weigh him in honest scales" for he knows that he is righteous (31: 6) – if he has sinned he is willing to accept God's punishment.

Job 32–37: Eliphaz, Bildad and Zophar give up responding to Job since they realise that they cannot convince him and so Elihu, the youngest of the group who has not previously spoken, speaks up. Having listened to the preceding discourse, Elihu is angry with Job for justifying himself rather than God (32: 2) and with the others for not persuading Job that he was wrong (32: 3, 12). Elihu then insists that God does speak though man may not perceive (33: 14) and so Job should not complain that God doesn't answer him (33: 13). Elihu gives some examples of how God speaks – both through dreams of warning (33: 15) and through inflicting pain by way of correction (33: 19). With prophetic words that predict the coming of Jesus, Elihu then refers to an 'angel' who mediates between humankind and God and therefore brings about humankind's restoration from the punishment for their sins (33: 23–30). Elihu next accuses Job of wickedness for insisting that he is innocent and God unjust (34: 5–9). Job cannot be correct since God is just (34: 10–12). Elihu then talks of God's impartiality (34: 18–19) and His judgement of wickedness (34: 21–28). Hence, Job must be sinful and is also rebellious in his accusations against God (34: 37). Job is insignificant compared to God as is his sinfulness or righteousness (35: 6). God does not listen to the cries of the wicked (35: 13) therefore God will not answer Job's wicked case against Him (35: 14). Elihu then makes the error of claiming to speak on behalf of God (36: 2). God exalts the righteous and punishes the wicked, explaining to the wicked why He has done so in order to help them to repent (36: 5–12). God is therefore trying to rescue Job from his wickedness (36: 16). Elihu concludes by describing God's power and asking Job to consider it (36: 22).

Job 38–40: 2: Following on from Elihu's speech, God enters the scene and answers Job "out of the storm" (38: 1). Perhaps it is the same storm that Elihu has just been describing using the imagery of lightning (37: 15). God acknowledges Job's desire to contend with Him and says, "I will question you and you shall answer me" (38: 3).

God then describes His might and power in contrast to that of Job. He is almost mocking in His manner as He describes His role as Creator and Sustainer of the universe (38: 4–39: 30) and so emphasises his distinctness to humankind. Whilst, at other points, God's words give a more intimate portrayal of the Creator's relationship with His creation as illustrated for example by His concern for a single doe giving birth to a fawn (39: 1–4). God concludes His speech with a challenge to Job to respond (40: 2).

Job 40: 3–5: Job replies that he is unworthy to speak to God and has no answer and so will be silent. Thus Job confirms his earlier view that, despite his yearning, it would actually be impossible to contend with God without some kind of intermediary

Job 40: 6–41: God says that He will continue to question Job (40: 7) and appears insulted that Job would question His justice (40: 8). God's questioning takes the form of Him contrasting His own power with that of Job. He does this primarily by describing His most fearful creations – Behemoth (40: 15–24) and Leviathan (41: 1–34). Therefore no-one can stand against God (41: 10).

Job 42: 1–7: Job then takes back what he said for, "I spoke of things I did not understand" (42: 3). Having seen God, Job repents (42: 6).

Job 42: 7–8: God then says that He is angry with Eliphaz, Bildad and Zophar and commands them to sacrifice a burnt offering as an act of repentance. God places Job in the role of intercessor for his friends and says that He will accept Job's prayers on their behalf (42: 8). God has therefore reversed the roles of Job and his friends who previously thought that they were intervening for Job on God's behalf. God also says that Job's friends have not spoken what is right but that Job has (42: 7). The book concludes with the restoration of Job to wealth that was in excess of his former riches.

God in Pain

# Bibliography

Baggini, Julian. *The Pig that wants to be eaten and ninety-nine other thought experiments*. London: Granta Books, 2005.

Blocher, Henri. *Evil and the Cross: An analytical look at the problem of pain*. Grand Rapids: Kregel Publications, 2004.

Boyd, Gregory. *Is God to Blame?* Eastbourne: Kingsway Publications, 2004.

Bradbury, Paul. *Life from Death Emerging*. London: Triangle, 2002.

Burgess, Anthony. *A Clockwork Orange*. London: Penguin Books, 2011.

Davis, Stephen T. (ed). *Encountering evil. Live options in theodicy. A new edition*. London: Westminster John Knox Press, 2001.

Flew, Antony. *Divine omnipotence and human freedom*, published in *New Essays in Philosophical Theology* edited by Antony Flew and Alasdair MacIntyre. New York: The MacMillan Company, 1966.

Forster, Roger. *Suffering and the Love of God*. London: PUSH Publishing, 2006.

Dostoevsky, Fyodor. *The Brothers Karamazov*. Translated by Richard Pevear and Larissa Volokhonsky. London: Vintage, 1992.

Hick, John. *Evil and the God of Love*. Basingstoke: Palgrave Macmillan, 2010.

Hume, David. *Dialogues and Natural History of Religion*. Oxford: Oxford University Press, 1993.

Keller, Timothy. *Walking with God through pain & suffering*. London: Hodder & Stoughton, 2013.

Klein, Stefan. *Survival of the Nicest. How Altruism Made Us Human and Why It Pays to Get Along*. London: Scribe, 2014.

LaCocque, André. *Justice for Innocent Job!*, *Biblical Interpretation*, vol. 19, no. 1, issue 1, 2011.

Lewis, C. S. *A Grief Observed*. London: Faber and Faber, 1966.

Lewis, C. S. *The Problem of Pain*. London: HarperCollinsPublishers, 2002.

Mackie, J.L. *Evil and Omnipotence*, *Mind*, vol. 64, no. 254, April 1955.

Metaxas, Eric, Socrates in the City. London: Collins, 2011.

Moltmann, Jürgen. *The Crucified God. The Cross of Christ as the Foundation and Criticism of Christian Theology*. London: SCM Press, 1974.

Moule, C. F. D. *Christ Alive and at Large. Unpublished writings of C F D Moule*. Norwich: Canterbury Press, 2010.

Moule, H. C. G. *The School of Suffering. A Brief Memorial of Mary E. E. Moule*. London: Society for Promoting Christian Knowledge, 1905.

Moule, H. C. G. *From Sunday to Sunday*. London: Isbister & Company Limited, 1903.

Plantinga, Alvin. *God, Freedom and Evil*. Grand Rapids: Wm. B. Eerdmans Publishing Company, 1977.

Voltaire. *Candide, or Optimism*. Translated by Theo Cuffe. London: Penguin Books, 2005.

Wiesel, Elie. *Night*. Translated by Marion Wiesel. London: Penguin Books, 2008.

Wiesel, Elie. *The Trial of God*. Translated by Marion Wiesel. New York: Schocken Books, 1995.

Wright, N. T. *Evil and the Justice of God*. London: Society for Promoting Christian Knowledge, 2006.

Wright, N. T. *Paul for everyone: Romans: Part 1: Chapters 1–8*. London: SPCK, 2004.

Yancey, Philip. *Disappointment with God.* London: Marshall Pickering, 1995.

# End notes

[1] Jürgen Moltmann, *The Crucified God*, page 201.

[2] Hume, *Dialogues and Natural History of Religion*, page 100, by permission of Oxford University Press.

[3] Hume, *Dialogues and Natural History of Religion*, page 103, by permission of Oxford University Press.

[4] Page 53. Taken from *Evil and the Cross* © Copyright 1994 by Henri Blocher. Published by Kregel Publications, Grand Rapids, MI. Used by permission of the publisher. All rights reserved.

[5] Page 85. Taken from *Evil and the Cross* © Copyright 1994 by Henri Blocher. Published by Kregel Publications, Grand Rapids, MI. Used by permission of the publisher. All rights reserved.

[6] Page 100. Taken from *Evil and the Cross* © Copyright 1994 by Henri Blocher. Published by Kregel Publications, Grand Rapids, MI. Used by permission of the publisher. All rights reserved.

[7] Hick, *Evil and the God of Love*, page 9, reproduced with permission of SCSC.

[8] Lewis, *The Problem of Pain*, pages XI-XII of preface.

[9] Lewis, *A Grief Observed*, page 27.

[10] Keller, *Walking with God through Pain & Suffering*, page 7. © 2013 Timothy Keller.

[11] Hume, *Dialogues and Natural History of Religion*, pages 95-115, by permission of Oxford University Press.

[12] Plantinga, *God, Freedom and Evil*, page 26. Please note that, since I have missed out many of Alvin Plantinga's statements, I have adopted a different numbering system and therefore used 'a' / 'b' rather than the 1 / 2 format that he uses. Hopefully this will prevent confusion between his

[13] Plantinga, quoted by Keller, *Walking with God through Pain & Suffering*, page 98. © 2013 Timothy Keller.

[14] Plantinga, *God, Freedom and Evil*, page 29.

[15] Hick, *Evil and the God of Love*, page 148f, reproduced with permission of SCSC.

[16] Leibniz is discussed in the chapter, *God intends all things for good*.

[17] Hick, *Evil and the God of Love*, page 153, reproduced with permission of SCSC.

[18]

http://onegoodmove.org/1gm/1gmarchive/2006/05/richard
_dawkins_3.html

[19] Davis, *Encountering Evil*, page 102.

[20] Page 100. Taken from *Evil and the Cross* © Copyright 1994 by Henri Blocher. Published by Kregel Publications, Grand Rapids, MI. Used by permission of the publisher. All rights reserved.

[21] HCG Moule, *From Sunday to Sunday*, page 55.

[22] Elie Wiesel, *Night*, page 5.

[23] Bradbury, *Life from Death Emerging*, page 102

[24] Bradbury, *Life from Death Emerging*, page 104.

[25] Blocher, *Evil and the Cross*, page 96.

[26] Hick, *Evil and the God of Love*, page 357, reproduced with permission of SCSC.

[27] Hick, *Evil and the God of Love*, page 354, reproduced with permission of SCSC.

[28] Hick, *Evil and the God of Love*, page 354, reproduced with permission of SCSC.

[29] Wright, *Paul for everyone: Romans: Part 1: Chapters 1-8*, page 161.

[30] Forster, *Suffering and the Love of God*, page 141.

[31] Described in the chapter, *The philosophers discuss*.

[32] Dostoevsky, *The Brothers Karamazov*, page 236.

[33] Dostoevsky, *The Brothers Karamazov*, page 237.

[34] *The Russian Herald* (1877, no. 9). Dostoevsky, *The Brothers Karamazov*, page 242, footnote 8.

[35] Dostoevsky, *The Brothers Karamazov*, page 244.

[36] Dostoevsky, *The Brothers Karamazov*, page 245.

[37] Hick, *Evil and the God of Love*, page 10, reproduced with permission of SCSC.

[38] Dostoevsky, *The Brothers Karamazov*, page 245.

[39] See the chapter *God intends all things for good?* for a further description of Voltaire's *Candide*.

[40] Wiesel, *Night*, page 34.

[41] Moule, *The School of Suffering. A Brief Memorial of Mary E. E. Moule*, page 72.

[42] Moule, *The School of Suffering. A Brief Memorial of Mary E. E. Moule*, page 48.

[43] Moule, *The School of Suffering. A Brief Memorial of Mary E. E. Moule*, page 109.

[44] Dostoevsky, *The Brothers Karamazov*, page 251.

[45] Dostoevsky, *The Brothers Karamazov*, page 254.

[46] Dostoevsky, *The Brothers Karamazov*, page 256.

[47] Dostoevsky, *The Brothers Karamazov*, page 257.

[48] Dostoevsky, *The Brothers Karamazov*, page 257.

[49] Dostoevsky, *The Brothers Karamazov*, page 260.

[50] Dostoevsky, *The Brothers Karamazov*, page 262.

[51] Dostoevsky, *The Brothers Karamazov*, page 262.

[52] Dostoevsky, *The Brothers Karamazov*, page 263.

[53] Plantinga, *God, Freedom, and Evil*, page 30.

[54] Baggini, *The Pig that wants to be eaten*, pages 283-5.

[55] Moltmann, *The Crucified God*, pages 62-63.

[56] I am making use here of Hick's discussion of *The Meaning of Evil* contained in *Evil and the Love of God*, pages 107-114.

[57] Hick, *Evil and the Love of God*, page 109, reproduced with permission of SCSC.

[58] Hick, *Evil and the Love of God*, page 108, reproduced with permission of SCSC.

[59] Flew & MacIntyre (ed), *New Essays in Philosophical Theology*, pages 144-169.

[60] Flew, *Divine omnipotence and human freedom*, page 149.

[61] Flew, *Divine omnipotence and human freedom*, page 149.

[62] Flew, *Divine omnipotence and human freedom*, page 153.

[63] Hick, *Evil and the God of Love*, page 272, reproduced with permission of SCSC.

[64] Davis, *Encountering Evil. Live Options in Theodicy*, page 77.

[65] La Cocque, *Justice for Innocent Job!*, page 21.

[66] George MacDonald, *Unspoken Sermons, First Series*, quoted by Lewis, *The Problem of Pain*, page VII.

[67] Lewis, *The Problem of Pain*, page 148.

[68] Voltaire, *Candide, or Optimism*, page 65.

[69] Voltaire, *Candide, or Optimism*, page 52.

[70] Davis, *Encountering Evil*, page 52.

[71] Pages 88-89. Taken from *Evil and the Cross* © Copyright 1994 by Henri Blocher. Published by Kregel Publications, Grand Rapids, MI. Used by permission of the publisher. All rights reserved.

[72] Moule, *Christ Alive and at Large*, page 98.

[73] Wright, *Evil and Justice of God*, page 5.

[74] Hick, *Evil and the God of Love*, page 11, reproduced with permission of SCSC.

[75] Hick, *Evil and the God of Love*, page 11, reproduced with permission of SCSC.

[76] Richard Dawkins, *The Selfish Gene*, (Oxford: Oxford University Press, 1989), page 2, quoted by Klein, *Survival of the Nicest. How Altruism Made Us Human and Why It*

*Pays to Get Along*, page 16.

[77] Hick, *Evil and the God of Love*, page 333, reproduced with permission of SCSC.

[78] Hick, *Evil and the God of Love*, page 375, reproduced with permission of SCSC.

[79] Davis, *Encountering Evil. Live Options in Theodicy*, page 87.

[80] Davis, *Encountering Evil. Live Options in Theodicy*, page 87.

[81] Forster, *Suffering and the Love of God*, page 69.

[82] Forster, *Suffering and the love of God*, pages 156-157.

[83] Davis, *Encountering Evil. Live Options in Theodicy*, pages 108-144.

[84] Davis, *Encountering Evil. Live Options in Theodicy*, page 108.

[85] Armstrong, *A History of God*, page 431.

[86] Wiesel, *The Trial of God*, page 172.

[87] Wiesel, *The Trial of God*, pages 128-9.

[88] Forster, *Suffering and the Love of God*, page 54.

[89] Moule, H.C.G., *From Sunday to Sunday*, pages 244-5.

[90] Bradbury, *Life from Death Emerging*, page 36.

[91] Hick, *Evil and the God of Love*, page 236, reproduced with permission of SCSC.

[92] Roth, *Encountering evil. Live options in theodicy* (Davis ed.), page 8.

[93] Forster, *Suffering and the love of God*, page 162.

[94] Boyd, *Is God to blame?*, pages 117-118.

[95] Boyd, *Is God to blame?*, page 117.

[96] Boyd, *Is God to blame?* page 118.

[97] Hick, *Evil and the God of Love*, page 104, reproduced with permission of SCSC.

[98] Hick, *Evil and the God of Love*, page 228, reproduced with permission of SCSC.

[99] Hick, *Evil and the God of Love*, page 290, reproduced

with permission of SCSC.

[100] Polkinghorne, *Socrates in the City* (Metaxas ed.), page 32.

[101] Davis, *Encountering Evil. Live Options in Theodicy*, page 87.

[102] Keller, *Walking with God through Pain and Suffering*, page 121. © 2013 Timothy Keller.

[103] Keller, *Walking with God through Pain and Suffering*, page 122. © 2013 Timothy Keller.

[104] Hick, *Evil and the God of Love*, page 243, reproduced with permission of SCSC.

[105] Page 132. Taken from *Evil and the Cross* © Copyright 1994 by Henri Blocher. Published by Kregel Publications, Grand Rapids, MI. Used by permission of the publisher. All rights reserved.

[106] Moule, C.F.D., *Christ Alive and at Large*, page 98.

[107] Wiesel, *Night*, page 66.

[108] Wright, *Evil and the Justice of God*, page 62.

[109] Leibniz, who is discussed in my chapter *God intends all things for good?* is therefore remarkable in his denial of this.

[110] Hume, *Dialogues and Natural History of Religion*, page 96, by permission of Oxford University Press.

[111] Hume, *Dialogues and Natural History of Religion*, page 99, by permission of Oxford University Press.

[112] Hume, *Dialogues and Natural History of Religion*, page 114, by permission of Oxford University Press.